living the
SPIRIT
FORMED
LIFE

JACK W. HAYFORD

Regal

A Division of Gospel Light
Ventura, California, U.S.A.

PUBLISHED BY REGAL BOOKS
FROM GOSPEL LIGHT
VENTURA, CALIFORNIA, U.S.A.
Regal   PRINTED IN THE U.S.A.

Regal Books is a ministry of Gospel Light, a Christian publisher dedicated to serving the local church. We believe God's vision for Gospel Light is to provide church leaders with biblical, user-friendly materials that will help them evangelize, disciple and minister to children, youth and families.

It is our prayer that this Regal book will help you discover biblical truth for your own life and help you meet the needs of others. May God richly bless you.

Revised and expanded edition. Originally published as *The Power and Blessing* by Victor Books in 1994. Portions of the book are adapted from Jack Hayford's *Prayer Path*, published by Tyndale House in 1984.

Spirit-Formed™ is a registered trademark.

Cover and Internal Design by Robert Williams
Edited by David Webb

Library of Congress Cataloging-in-Publication Data
Hayford, Jack W.
    Living the Spirit-formed life / Jack W. Hayford.
        p.   cm.
    ISBN 0-8307-2767-1 (trade paper)
    1. Spiritual life—Christianity.   I. Title.

BV4501.3 .H39   2001
248.4—dc21   2001019073

2 3 4 5 6 7 8 9 10 11 12 13 14 15 / 12 11 10 09 08 07 06 05 04

Rights for publishing this book in other languages are contracted by Gospel Light Worldwide, the international nonprofit ministry of Gospel Light. Gospel Light Worldwide also provides publishing and technical assistance to international publishers dedicated to producing Sunday School and Vacation Bible School curricula and books in the languages of the world. For additional information, visit www.gospellightworldwide.org; write to Gospel Light Worldwide, P.O. Box 3875, Ventura, CA 93006; or send an e-mail to info@gospellightworldwide.org.

CONTENTS

Prologue. 7
Spirit-Fullness and Timelessness

Part I
The Spirit-Formed Disciple

The Making of a Disciple. 13
The Pillar Principle

Part II
The Disciplines of the Spirit

Fundamentals of the Spirit-Formed Life. 21
As Time Goes By

The First Discipline 25
Committing to Hear God's Voice

The Second Discipline 43
Living in the Power of Baptism

The Third Discipline 57
Celebrating the Lord's Table

The Fourth Discipline 71
Walking in the Spirit of Forgiveness

The Fifth Discipline 85
Feeding on the Word of God

The Sixth Discipline 95
Maintaining Integrity of Heart

The Seventh Discipline 117
Abiding in the Fullness of the Spirit

The Eighth Discipline 133
Living a Life of Submission

The Ninth Discipline 151
Practicing Solitude

The Tenth Discipline 171
Living as a Worshiper

Part III
The Discipline of Prayer

Above and Beneath It All 193
Walking the Path of Prayer

Prayer Path: Step 1 195
Confident Faith

Prayer Path: Step 2 201
Transforming Faith

Prayer Path: Step 3 207
Responsible Faith

Prayer Path: Step 4 213
Dependent Faith

Prayer Path: Step 5 217
Releasing Faith

Prayer Path: Step 6 223
Obedient Faith

Prayer Path: Step 7 227
Trusting Faith

Prayer Path: Step 8 233
Jesus' Lessons on Bold Faith

Prayer Path: Step 9 243
Prayer That Intervenes and Reverses

Prayer Path: Step 10 257
The Practice of Fasting

Epilogue of Encouragement 269
Beyond Disciplines

Appendix 1 285
How to Receive the Fullness of the Holy Spirit

Appendix 2 287
Resources for Further Study of the Disciplines

Endnotes 297

SPIRIT-FULLNESS AND TIMELESSNESS

*My little children, for whom I labor in birth again until
Christ is formed in you.*

GALATIANS 4:19

This is an invitation to adventure. You hold in your hands a handbook designed to help serious Christians find fulfillment in life and maturity under Christ's lordship by linking their souls to timeless practices and principles set forth in Scripture and proven valid.

Mind you, the adventure I speak of is neither a spartan excursion nor an amusement-park ride. I say this because I have sought to make the disciplines of the Christian life accessible without seeming trivial.

You see, although I have benefited greatly from my exploration of contemporary books on spiritual discipline, nevertheless they tend to be the kind of heavy reading that intimidates most earnest believers. I think this is because the disciplines have sometimes been reduced to a legalistic form of demanding, exacting accomplishment.

Further, the pursuit of these disciplines has often been measured by the patterns established by the saints of earlier centuries. Whatever value we may draw from these spiritual giants— and there is a great deal to be learned and much wisdom to be acquired from them—these men were living in a world with radically different schedules, pressures and demands. Their writings on issues of discipline were lengthy, but often in their monastic or mystic lifestyles they had little else to occupy their thoughts.

I have sought with this book to be concise and personal, hopefully without being too "here and now." I realize this might strike the elite disciplinarian as shallow; but if it does, my hope is that he or she will pursue the abundance of other materials I have written and taught on these grand themes. And so, to the task of becoming a deepened disciple *in the present hour*.

Just as the dawn of the twentieth century marked an outpouring of the Holy Spirit upon spiritually hungry souls, the turn of the twenty-first century is witness to a new dimension of passion for God. The quest of those earlier seekers was satisfied, and their witness has spanned a century and helped to shape Christian history. Today we surge forward in the wake of this holy stream of grace that has been experienced from Azusa Street to the far corners of the earth.

This global spread of Christ-exalting evangelism and Spirit-empowered ministry has been advanced by the positive impact of Christian media—radio, television and publishing. But simultaneously, a gradual shift in focus toward success or entertainment in these media, often mixed with a quick-fix or bless-me centeredness, has produced confusion about what Spirit-filled, Spirit-formed living is really about.

The call to the Spirit-formed life defines the normal Christian life as conceived by our Lord Jesus Christ. It is the kind of life, experience and witness that is described in the book of Acts. Indeed, the steps forward to the Holy Spirit-formed life are clearly set forth in God's Word:

1. Be *Spirit-born* by repenting for your sins and by putting your faith in Jesus Christ as your *Savior*, verifying the commitment by obeying Jesus Christ as *Lord* and being baptized in water (see Acts 2:38,39).
2. Be *Spirit-filled* by receiving the promise Jesus gave that

His followers shall receive power—power to move in new dimensions of worship, praise, prayer, service and witness (see Acts 1:5-8; 2:1-4).

3. Be *Spirit-formed* by recognizing that the entry door of new birth and the birthright blessing of Holy Spirit fullness are only *beginnings*—both calling us as believers to *growth* in Christ's likeness and *discipleship* under His lordship (see Rom. 12:1,2; Acts 2:42,46,47).

It is the apostolic heart cry of Paul, Peter and John that all believers are called to the Spirit-filled life, whether they are born in the first or the twenty-first century.

Stop indulging in transient style and stimulation. Instead, keep on being filled with the Holy Spirit, as you sing and worship the Lord from your hearts, and as you live in timeless gratitude to God in Jesus' name, and as you relate to each other in a climate of mutual submission to God's wisdom and order (Eph. 5:18-21, author's paraphrase).

Every generation since the Church was born has been called to an abiding lifestyle that learns God's grace but lives Christ's laws. This is called being a disciple. Christian discipleship consists of those life principles that beget a timeless quality in the life of the believer. It is the *practical* aspect of eternal life, lived in the here and now, in contrast with the *promised* aspect of eternal life, which we will enjoy then and there, forever in God's presence.

Our generation of believers has now crossed over the line into Century 21, and I have a deep, joyous sense about it. I believe this new era is the one in which we will experience the setting in place of the new reformation. By this I mean that we will see the global Church filled with people who not only are settled in the solid, biblical realities of the unshakeable truths regarding

Jesus Christ, His person and work, as achieved through His life, death and resurrection; but we will also see a full recovery of the kind and quality of life in Christ that is characterized by all the passion and power of true Holy Spirit-fullness.

Are you a church leader, worker or member seeking freshness and power in your life? Are you looking for more than either the formal or the flamboyant, the painfully predictable or the merely excitable? Do you want more of Christ and the freedom to move in the life of His Holy Spirit? Then join me in answering the call to Spirit-filled *disciplines* as well as Spirit-filled *dynamics*.

When the power life is linked to the disciplined life, we will have overthrown any misinterpretation of what being filled with the Spirit means; and we will have reaffirmed the timeless lifestyle that has always been foundational to renewal, revival or anointing—true Spirit-fullness. We will have entered a new era of the Church where lines of separation—differences over Pentecostal experience, evangelical solidity, charismatic passion and fundamentalist purity—will gradually disappear.

I believe this new era will be hastened in direct proportion to the Spirit-fullness manifested among those of us who seek full-dimensional spirituality—

where Jesus Christ is exalted and is central in all,

where God's Word is honored and authoritative in all,

where the Holy Spirit is welcomed and free to work in every way and

where spiritual dynamics and spiritual disciplines are joined by all.

What a time! What a goal!

Join me. Let's go for all of it!

In Jesus' name, His life and His love,
Jack W. Hayford

Part One

THE
SPIRIT-FORMED
DISCIPLE

Fear not that thy life shall come to an end, but rather
fear that it shall never have a beginning.

JOHN HENRY NEWMAN
1801-1890

Ask not for gifts but for the Giver of Gifts: not for life
but for the Giver of Life—then life and the things needed for life
will be added unto you.

SADHU SUNDAR SINGH
INDIAN EVANGELIST
1889-1929

THE PILLAR PRINCIPLE

He who overcomes, I will make him a pillar in the temple of My
God. . . . I will write on him the name of My God.

REVELATION 3:12

As we begin our pursuit to deepen our discipleship as followers of Jesus Christ, it's more than merely imaginable that some readers will feel doubtful about their capacity to rise to the dimensions of maturity one might expect to see in a settled servant of the Savior. Before we proceed any further, lay hold of this: If ever you may be tempted to doubt or to wonder about your potential as a disciple, take a good look at Simon Peter.

There's a reason Peter is a favorite of almost every reader of the Bible. His stumblings seem to summarize the sum and substance (or lack of it) we all frequently feel about our own feeble steps as we attempt to move forward in Christ! Consider these extremes. With one utterance—"You are the Christ, the Son of the living God" (Matt. 16:16)—Simon Peter rises to the highest heights of insight and declaration. Then, just moments later, Jesus denounces another of Peter's "insights" as satanic in origin, saying, "You are an offense to Me, for you are not mindful of the things of God, but the things of men" (v. 23). (Such a thing should never happen to you!) On the night of Jesus' capture, Peter declares, "I will never fail you!" (see Mark 14:29). But within hours he denies three times even knowing his Lord.

As we look over Peter's life as a disciple, we see him as both a saint and sinner, a spiritual giant and spiritual dwarf. But in the end, we are touched and encouraged, because he is so much like us. He is everyman wrapped into a single person. He's the reflection of our secret ambitions fulfilled and the picture of our visible embarrassments revisited. Yet at whatever point we see him in the span or spectrum of his exploits or his flops, whether at a pinnacle or a pratfall, Peter inevitably ends up at the right place, showing the right attitudes and aiming in the right direction en route to the right goal.

It's the *end* of Simon Peter's "becoming" that finally captures our hearts. He fumbles the ball, but he also picks it up and runs for a touchdown. He is decidedly *not* the person described by the modern-day concept that employs his name (but is actually named after the man who coined the term). The Peter Principle describes the corporate businessperson who rises within an organization to reach a point beyond his or her competence. Our man is quite the opposite. *This* Peter—Simon Peter—continued growing as a committed disciple, and he matured through and *beyond* his apparent limitations. He became a *pillar*—a tower of strength in his own generation.

That's why I've come to think of Simon Peter as the Bible's Rocky—not only because his name means the same thing (the Greek *petras* = "rock"), but because there are a number of similarities between the big fisherman of history and the fictional boxer portrayed by Sylvester Stallone in a popular movie series. Both are rough, unpolished men. Both are products of a distinct ethnicity. Both are laden with undeveloped potential (until trainers get hold of them). Both end up finding their possibilities maximized, and they rise to the level of a champion.

Peter is some kind of a person!

But so are you! That's a proposition Peter himself asserted in his first letter (call it 1 Peter or Rocky 1, take your pick). There we find Holy Spirit-inspired words that breathe hope and promise for every one of us who would become maturing disciples. Doubtless remembering how Jesus had first prophesied that he would be called a stone (see John 1:42), Peter harkens to the day Jesus leveled His gaze, looked deep into his eyes and said, "I say to you that you *are* Peter!" (Matt. 16:18, emphasis added). Moved by these memories of what Jesus had processed in his life, Peter declares something about every believer's potential as a disciple: "You also, as living stones, are being built up a spiritual house" (1 Pet. 2:5).

In light of these words of promise—words of prophecy—the Bible holds a similar word for us from Jesus Himself. Just as Peter's experience speaks to you and me and points the way to the possibilities that Christ can bring about in our lives, so Jesus adds His own "pillar" promise:

> He who overcomes, I will make him a pillar in the temple of My God, and he will not go out from it anymore (Rev. 3:12, *NASB*).

Here we are introduced to the elements of the Master's program for exceeding man's Peter Principle with God's Pillar Principle; it gives us reason to believe we can pursue growth as disciples without being plagued with doubt as to whether we're dreaming beyond reality. Christ's words outline His program: *faith* ("he who overcomes"), *creative power* ("I will make him") and *stability* ("a pillar"). To understand these words is to believe.

FAITH

Faith isn't demanded in giant proportions but only as a basic, foundational trust in Jesus—that is, faith in who He is and confidence in what He has done for us as mankind's only Savior. That is how the Bible defines "overcoming":

For whatever is born of God overcomes the world. And this is the victory that has overcome the world—our faith. Who is he who overcomes the world, but he who believes that Jesus is the Son of God? (1 John 5:4,5).

So to begin, the question is settled as to your or my candidacy as a disciple—a potential pillar. Our commitment to Jesus as Savior opens the door: Salvation plants the seed of eternal life inside of us, and within that seed is a holy DNA destined to grow us into Christ's likeness.

CREATIVE POWER

Awesome creative power is promised in Jesus' words "I will make him a pillar." Here Jesus speaks in terms totally opposite those of human programs and philosophies of self-help and self-cultivation-unto-achievement. He doesn't say, "*You can* make it happen." He says, "*I will* make it happen."

"I will make him a pillar," He says. Especially moving to me is the meaning of the word used in this passage. The word "make" encompasses both ideas—the shaping of something already present, but also *bringing into existence anything that is needed but lacking*. In short, Jesus is saying, "I'm going to take the raw material of your life and shape it. But if you're concerned that what you lack will hinder My work, don't be afraid. I can *create* things in you that don't yet exist!"

"I will make him a pillar." Equally significant to the meaning of this phrase is that the future tense of a Greek verb conveys the idea of continuous action. Our Lord promises, "I will keep on making, creating and shaping until your possibilities are developed—until My pillar project is completed." This is His way of saying, "I've got the will and the power if you've got the willingness and the availability."

STABILITY

He's talking about making a *pillar*—a strong support to others, an architecturally strategic column upon which structures lean and find strength. He's talking about making me into a father my kids can lean on, a husband my wife can trust and a friend my associates know won't fail them. Whatever your gender or your circle of influence, He means to do the same with you: faithful church worker, dependable employee, loving spouse, wise parent, good pastor, considerate boss, helpful neighbor, etc. Jesus is in the business of making pillars—that is, producing a settled stability that will bring an end to vacillation and undependability in us as surely as it did in Simon Peter.

So step up to examine the disciplines of the Spirit-formed life. Be encouraged that you're

The interior journey of the soul from the wilds of sin into the enjoyed presence of God is beautiful. Ransomed men need no longer pause in fear before the Holy of Holies. God wills that we should push on into His presence and live our whole life there.

A. W. TOZER
1897-1963

moving forward in a process that holds the hope of fruitfulness and fulfillment, because it happened in another person very like us—a man named Peter. Because the New Testament traces Jesus' dealings with Simon Peter, who became a pillar in the end, we can believe.

Jesus Christ is still in the pillar-forming business. It's a principle of His—the Pillar Principle. His Pillar Principle declares, "I can and I will take those who put abiding faith in Me, and I will make them into dependable disciples—people who will prove to be strategic in My ongoing work of building My Church!"

Part Two

THE
DISCIPLINES
OF THE SPIRIT

The surest symbol of a heart not yet fully subdued to God and His will is going to be found in the areas of money, sex and power: in wanting these things for ourselves. The surest symbol of spiritual earnestness will be the checkbook, the affections and the ego-drive surrendered to Him. A disciple must have discipline. He must not be afraid of being asked by God for some of the time, the money and the pleasure he has been in the habit of calling his "own." This does not mean that there will not be time for the family and time for some healthy diversion. But it does mean that we are never—on vacation, or wherever we may be—exempt from our primary commitment to Him.

SAMUEL SHOEMAKER
1893-1963

As Time Goes By

Something almost nasty distilled around the word "fundamental" during the latter half of the twentieth century, and it's too bad that happened.

This unfortunate vilification of the word was the collective result of a number of things, any one of which would probably not have been enough to cause the semidemise of the word's acceptability but which, joined together, have all but killed it.

For example, fundamentals are unpopular in education. New, "creative" approaches to classroom curricula and teaching may have sounded bright and snappy when they were proposed. But in recent years our educational system has produced a deprived generation, nearly half of which is virtually illiterate. The same observation could be made in any number of fields of labor or study, in which the fundamentals have been decried as stodgy—uninteresting to a person who wants to enter a field of work but has no desire to dig deep enough to find the roots of what grows there.

And, of course, the word "fundamentalist" has become a public media epithet—a cuss word meaning Christians who believe in such things as God the Creator, Jesus the Savior, the Bible as God's Word, the reality of the Holy Spirit, heaven, hell and other such "invisibles."

But whatever negative notions have been conjured up around the idea of fundamentals, there is no way life can be lived successfully without finding and applying them, whatever your field of interest. Like the pop song of another generation says, "The fundamental things apply, as time goes by."[1]

That's what this section of the book presents: fundamental things that through their careful application have proven indispensable to spiritual growth, as time goes by.

There are two important things to know as you enter into this portion of our study: (1) the *reason* for the disciplines we will discuss and (2) the *spirit* of our approach.

The *reason* for selecting the 10 specific disciplines to be discussed has to do with my perspective, and mine alone. They are matters that have come to matter most to me. I've focused on these few basics, because I think they determine the climate of a soul—if these things are pursued, everything else will grow.

The *spirit* of my approach is nontechnical and insistently practical—what I like to call incarnational. By that, I refer to my conviction that God is not so interested in educating us as He is in *transforming* us. The call to be a disciple is ultimately a matter of "Christ in you, the hope of glory" (Col. 1:27). The 10 disciplines presented here help us to experience ongoing transformation into the image of Jesus (see 2 Cor. 3:18).

One last comment: I don't know how anyone could make an authoritative determination as to the order of priority in which these disciplines should be listed. Perhaps it's immaterial. They aren't *observed* in a sequence but, rather, we live and make progress in all of them at the same time. So you may prioritize them as you wish, but please, don't allow that to reduce the importance of any one of them in your lifestyle as a disciple.

Now that we've taken a fundamental look at our fundamental need for a fundamentally disciplined walk with Christ, let's proceed!

The real problem of the Christian life comes where people do not usually look for it. It comes the very moment you wake up each morning. All your wishes and hopes for the day rush at you like wild animals. And the first job each morning consists simply in shoving them all back; in listening to that other Voice, taking that other point of view, letting that other larger, stronger, quieter life come flowing in. And so on, all day.

C. S. LEWIS, 1900-1963

PRINCIPLE

To read and study God's Word is to lay the foundation for all understanding and growth as a disciple of Jesus Christ. However, the Bible is a living Word that has not been given to us solely for information, analysis and education. God wants to speak to each one of His children—to teach and correct, to lead and direct, to keep and protect. For this to take place vitally and continuously, the believer needs to learn to hear His word within the Word—to receive the prophetic intent of the Holy Spirit breathing truth into our hearts in order to transform our lives.

PRACTICE

With full honor to the finality and the authority of the holy Scriptures in God's Word, the Bible, I offer in this chapter a story of my introduction to the decisive issue of *hearing* what is in His Word. To learn may bring intellectual knowledge through information; to hear will bring experiential knowledge through transformation.

COMMITTING TO HEAR GOD'S VOICE

My sheep hear My voice, and I know them, and they follow Me.

JOHN 10:27

I have chosen to begin my listing of the disciplines of the Spirit with a call to commit to hearing God's voice. My reason for selecting this starting place is simple: That's the way we *began* our life in Him!

Whatever testimony any of us bears in relating our joy for having received the gospel of Jesus Christ and being born again by the power of the Holy Spirit, our story begins someplace where, in some way, God "spoke" to us. He may have spoken through our circumstances. We may have received an internal, overwhelming sense of our need of Him, perhaps through dismal failure or discouragement. We may have heard Him through the witness of a friend, a broadcast, a piece of literature, by reading the Bible or simply through a passing observation. But something—*Someone!*—spoke to us, and we began to turn toward Him.

Over the years I have been impressed with the frequency of hearing from individuals who were spoken to long before they ever came to the Lord. They will remember hearing an inner voice in childhood or during a crisis long past—a "voice" that made them aware of their need and caused them to feel guilt, knowing they had violated a higher power. There are innumerable ways God deals with people even before they come to Christ, so it shouldn't surprise us that He so often speaks to His own redeemed children personally and intimately.

A Truth Celebrated in Song

Hearing God's voice has been something unapologetically acknowledged throughout the history of the Church, so much so that it has found a frequent thread in the hymns sung by the people of the Lord. Among the beloved classics widely sung in this century is:

> I come to the garden alone,
> While the dew is still on the roses,
> And the voice I hear falling on my ear,
> The Son of God discloses.
>
> And He walks with me, and He talks with me,
> And He tells me I am His own.
> And the joy we share as we tarry there,
> None other has ever known.[1]

The second verse of the same hymn describes "the sound of His voice" and expresses the individual's gratitude for the personal gift of a heart song given by the Savior: "The melody that He gave to me within my heart is ringing."

And who can forget the uncluttered liberty of a preceeding generation which rose to testify in song every Easter:

> He lives, He lives! Christ Jesus lives today!
> He walks with me and talks with me
> Along life's narrow way.
> He lives! He lives, salvation to impart!
> You ask me how I know He lives?
> He lives within my heart![2]

Until recent years, there was no segment of the living Church—none in the born-again community—that even questioned the matter of people hearing God's voice. Of course, there have always been rare, isolated cases of fantasy and error—always peculiar or even sad instances of individuals straying far or foolishly and claiming, "God told me to do this." But their ignorance, error or folly is not an argument against the biblically valid experience of hearing the voice of God.

So what brought about the curiosity of recent years—a small handful of evangelical Christian leaders attacking the idea that God still speaks today directly to people, especially His own redeemed?

THE CONCLUSIVE REVELATION

Well, the answer seems to be fear—fear that if they allow believers to expect God to speak to them, they may begin to hear voices and accept them as a substitute for, or as an addition to, the Bible. And since the conclusive revelation of God's Word in the 66 books of the Holy Bible *is* final and *is* complete, they view any expectation of hearing from God other than through the Bible as an inappropriate attitude that treats the Scriptures as being insufficient.

But this judgment will never be justified on the basis of anything we are discussing in our study of the spiritual disciplines and certainly not by our handling of God's Word. The preciousness and absolute authority of the Word of God is central to our life and tradition, and this is the case with many millions who, on and under the Bible's authority, *often* hear the voice of God speaking within their hearts.

Sometimes He speaks instructively, correctively, directively or protectively. Sometimes He speaks with thoughts we sense are

His, as the Holy Spirit ignites what we are reading from the pages of the Bible. Sometimes He speaks with inner promptings that come as divinely given intuition, insight or warning. Sometimes He speaks with prophetic words which draw our attention to a larger, clearer understanding of His will as revealed in His eternal Word.

But *always* He speaks on the basis that we know, love, study and search the Scriptures. They are our source of sufficiency as far as truth and wisdom are concerned, for in them is life and in them is protection against confusion or the possibility of error.

To liberate our minds from the fear of deception, however, every believer should be settled on the issue of avoiding, indeed of rejecting, any ideas of *continuing revelation*—the fallacious idea that the Bible isn't the final authority concerning God's revealed will and truth. It *is*, and we should never listen to anyone who argues otherwise where matters of spiritual life and truth are concerned. But there is still the truth that God does "reveal" things to His children today. Ephesians 1:17-23 notes how the Holy Spirit—the Giver of the Word—continues to minister to us in ways that enlighten our hearts to the hope the Father has given us and to the power available to bring it all to pass! However, every believer needs to know that this kind of revelation is in no way the equivalent of the "closed canon of the Scriptures," words which refer to the understanding that the Bible is a *finished* book.

The implications of this are clear:

1. There are not, nor ever will be, any other books, verses or ideas added to the Bible or placed beside it as equal in authority or revelation.
2. All preaching, teaching, prophesying or any other communication being declared in the name of the

Lord is to be subject to measurement by the content of the Word of God.

God Has Been Speaking

Once the truth regarding the absolute and final authority of the Scriptures is established, it is surprising to me that anyone would resist the idea that God still speaks to people in other ways today. God has been speaking to people from the beginning of human history, both directly and indirectly.

There are at least seven ways God speaks, and has spoken to, humankind.

- He speaks through creation's artistry and majesty with such a clarity that all humankind is held accountable to believe in the Creator (see Ps. 19:1-6; Rom. 1:20).
- He speaks through the moral sense placed in the human conscience, so that a fundamental sense of right and wrong is innately present (see Rom. 2:14,15).
- He speaks through the evidential instances of divine providence that affect our lives and speak to our souls (see Gen. 28:10-17; Acts 16:7).
- He speaks through signs and wonders or prophetic promptings by the Holy Spirit, and by these means He often convinces hearts of His power and presence (see 2 Kings 2:15; Acts 13:12; 1 Cor. 14:5,22-26).
- He speaks through the still small voice of God that sometimes addresses people within their hearts (see 1 Kings 11:12; Isa. 30:21; Acts 10:9-12).
- He speaks through His authoritative Word, the Holy Scriptures (see 2 Tim. 3:14-17), which He has given to

us through prophets and apostles by the Holy Spirit
(see 2 Pet. 1:19-21).

· He has spoken, ultimately and gloriously, through His
Son, Jesus Christ, the living Word of God who has
declared to us the Father's love for us and the saving
way by which we may return to Him (see John 14:1-12;
Heb. 1:1-4).

These ways, however, only remind us that (1) we only know these
are valid ways God speaks to us *because the Bible says so* and (2) we
are to measure what we perceive God speaks *only by the Bible's full
teaching and authority.*

God still speaks in all the same ways He always has: He is the
changeless God, and His reach to humankind continually
extends by every communicative means, including intimately
speaking by the Holy Spirit with His own sons and daughters in
Christ.

So in this light I welcome you to receive the first discipline:
committing to hearing God's voice. At a later point we will look
at our practices of regular Bible reading, study, memorization
and the quoting of promises as we mine all the riches of God's
Word. But to begin in ways that open us to His instruction as we
pursue *all* the disciplines and the freedom and joyfulness they
can bring to our lives, let us deal first with the sensitizing of our
hearing—having ears to hear.

Open your Bible to Mark 4. Lay it side by side with this book
and let us study together what I believe is the most important
truth concerning the use of God's Word: Jesus' lesson on listening.

The principal truth we will witness in this passage is the
absolute importance of *hearing* the words of the Bible. But hearing as evinced by Jesus has much more to do with an attitude a
Christian disciple must have than it does with one's ability to

hear the sounds of words and understand their meanings. Before we look closer at Mark 4, read the following passages:

> Therefore lay aside all filthiness and overflow of wickedness, and receive with meekness the implanted word, which is able to save your souls. But be doers of the word, and not hearers only, deceiving yourselves. For if anyone is a hearer of the word and not a doer, he is like a man observing his natural face in a mirror; for he observes himself, goes away, and immediately forgets what kind of man he was. But he who looks into the perfect law of liberty and continues in it, and is not a forgetful hearer but a doer of the work, this one will be blessed in what he does (Jas. 1:21-25).

> So then faith comes by hearing, and hearing by the word of God (Rom. 10:17).

These passages make it clear that hearing has to do with (1) a person's willingness to be *changed* by what he or she hears and (2) a living faith—not merely belief but the power to *see things changed*—that comes from this kind of hearing. In short, our willingness to be changed by the truth of the Word of God determines our ability to see things changed around us by the power of applying the Word's promises. With that in mind, let's examine Jesus' teaching about truly hearing the Word—the foremost expression of the voice of God.

A Strategic Encounter

Nothing has become more of a strategic point in my own spiritual journey than an encounter I had one day with the Holy

Spirit while opening the Bible for study. I had been progressing through the book of Mark, outlining each chapter for a teaching assignment, when I came to the fourth chapter.

My outline for this chapter progressed nicely:

1. The setting, verses 1 and 2
2. The sower parable, verses 3-9
3. The disciples' question, verses 10-12
4. The Lord's explanation, verses 13-20

At that point I came to the words of Mark 4:21-25:

> And He said to them, "Is a lamp brought to be put under a basket or under a bed? Is it not to be set on a lamp-stand? For there is nothing hidden which will not be revealed, nor has anything been kept secret but that it should come to light. If anyone has ears to hear, let him hear."
>
> And He said to them, "Take heed what you hear. With the same measure you use, it will be measured to you; and to you who hear, more will be given. For whoever has, to him more will be given; but whoever does not have, even what he has will be taken away from him."

As I paused to determine how to describe these five verses in my outline, I was stymied. These verses seemed to have little continuity or connection with the rest of the chapter. The five verses appeared to me to be unrelated to each other, as though they were a series of proverbs, meaning something like:

v. 21—Let your light shine for God.
v. 22—Better be good. Somebody's going to know how

you *really* lived when God shows the video of your secret life for all to see when you stand before Him someday.

v. 23—This seemed a kind of "amen" that might fit anywhere.

v. 24—Look out what you do to others, because you're going to get the same right back!

v. 25—Life's tough: The rich get richer and the poor get poorer.

I'll make no defense of my candid commentary, for to my eyes that particular day the passage was simply a collection of sayings with an "Amen!" in the middle. But knowing that God's Word is more coherent than it appeared in my superficial reading of these words, I stopped.

I prayed.

Kneeling beside the place where I was sitting, I said, "Holy Spirit, I know there must be a reason for these words in verses 21-25. Will You help me understand it?"

Instantly, these words flashed on my mind: *The candle is the parable.* I had been answered so quickly I could hardly contain myself!

I went back and read verse 21, and the light dawned: This verse was a direct follow-up to Jesus' explanation of the parable to His disciples. In short, having explained the parable of the sower in detail, Jesus goes on to say, "After all, isn't a lamp meant to shed light?" He's saying to his followers, "I'm using these parables, these picture stories, to be sure no one misses the point. So if you don't get the point, *ask.*" Verse 22 elaborates His desire that His disciples listen, learn and understand with clarity. Jesus essentially says, "There isn't anything that's been secret until now that I won't reveal to you! I want you to *know*."

THE CENTRAL POINT

Then comes the stinger, the point: "He who has ears to hear, let him hear." And it's right *there* that the Master's words issue time-less terms for knowing God's Word—*really* knowing it: *You have to be a genuine listener!*

That's what "having ears to hear" means. The Greek verb *akouo* refers to more than hearing sounds; it also refers to a per-son's *receiving* and *responding* to what he or she has heard. Thereby we see how Jesus' next words become so dramatically decisive.

"Take heed what you hear," the Savior warns. Then He adds, "Only to the degree you *hear* [receive and respond] will you be able to experience what God has for you." The issue is that you and I must respond to truth—not simply learn it.

The Lord summarizes His demanding provisos, saying, "Whoever *has* [that is, ears to hear, or a will to receive and respond to the truth the Holy Spirit reveals to him or her] shall receive *more*." Then He adds a frightening consequence for those who are unresponsive to God's Word: "Whoever does *not* have [whoever is capable of hearing the sounds but does not respond to the truth of the Word] will eventually lose what they originally had!"

Can you see why I was so moved to find the key to this series of verses?

What a towering truth! What powerfully poignant observa-tions Jesus makes on the dangers of being *around* the living Word and yet not responding, allowing the Word to fall on our ears only as optional pieces of information rather than as required hearing for personal *change*.

In this light, let's look again at the whole passage. Be-ginning at Mark 4:3, note Jesus' call: "Listen!" He is not merely attempting to gain the crowd's attention. This is a command to discipline our souls toward a constantly receptive, responsive stance when the living Word speaks. The parable that follows is far more than a simplistic description of the process of evangelistic preaching. It's a personal message to *all* of us for *all* our lives.

Every time God's Word is heard or read, we are accountable to Him for that privilege. Don't let the seed of truth fall on a barren heart, on stony attitudes or on weed-riddled terrain of a mind so preoccupied with temporal things that it's lost sight of things eternal.

Every time we hear a sermon or open the Scriptures, our assignment is to tune our souls to a readiness to be shaped, taught, corrected or advised. If I come with a closed agenda, presuming *I know this stuff already*, I'm on the brink of a distinct path toward eventual spiritual bankruptcy: "Whoever does not have, even what he has will be taken from him."

Understanding this text also clarifies the seemingly peculiar words of Jesus in verse 11:

> And He said to them, "To you it has been given to know the mystery of the kingdom of God; but to those who are outside, all things come in parables."

A casual reading of this verse almost sounds as though Jesus were intentionally trying to make it difficult for the multitude to understand Him. But clarity comes when we remember the broader context of His ministry at this point.

You see, Jesus had been ministering for many months in the regions around Galilee. He had made a complete circuit of towns and villages, with the crowds gathering to witness the miracles—the power ministry of the kingdom of God.

As He was about to start another preaching circuit of the area, "He began to teach by the sea" (Mark 4:1). But on this

A spiritual life without discipline is impossible. Discipline is the other side of discipleship. The practice of a spiritual discipline makes us more sensitive to the small, gentle voice of God.

HENRY J. M.
NOUWEN
1932-

round, He would require more response—more willingness to be changed and not just to watch.

Here there's a lesson in human nature and Jesus' way of dealing with it. He chose this time to begin using these story-lessons, or parables, to emphasize His teaching. Until that time, crowds had gathered to revel in the wonder of miracles and to rejoice in the gospel of forgiveness. Now, though Jesus would maintain constant the power manifest and the love offered, He would increase the requirement of a responsible response among hearers of His message.

So when the disciples asked, Jesus preceded His exposition with an explanation: "I'll show you the parable's meaning. These things are for your understanding." Then He presents a contrast. He notes the difference between those who are willing to be discipled and those who are only along for the ride. He says, "But to those who are *outside*" (that is, outside the circle of a will to accept the call to discipleship—to *following* Him, not just gathering for the miracles and the introductory things of the gospel), "these things come in parables." So we learn that Jesus' use of parables wasn't meant to puzzle people, but *to make the message so clear that nobody ever need misunderstand!* (Or if they did, their asking would find a willing and ready answer.)

Jesus goes on to quote Isaiah's prophecy (see Isa. 6:9,10) and apply it to His ministry. Some have thought these words in verse 12 were a statement of some divine intent to *make* people misunderstand. Instead, He was essentially acknowledging what we have already, that the crowds were eager for excitement but not for change. Essentially He says, "These *see* the truth, but they won't let it penetrate their vision. They *hear* it, but they won't grant an understanding response." Jesus quotes the prophet in explaining why people don't *really* listen. He said it was "Lest they should turn"—that is, turn to God's ways and be changed through the transforming power of "their sins [being] forgiven them." Jesus was noting how much human nature doesn't want to submit to change. We prefer *not* being untangled (forgiven) from sins we would rather embrace!

LISTENING UNTO FRUITFULNESS

Can you see, dear one, why this foundational lesson on how God's Word is to be approached is so very, very important? Here is a most sobering warning against passivity, presumption, indifference or a stolid predisposition that suggests *I already understand this* or *I have this down pat* or *I'm right and I know it and nothing or no one is going to change my mind!*

But there is also a glorious promise here.

In contrast to a human disposition toward self-will or stubborn pride, Jesus describes the certainty of a holy fruitfulness whereby a person responds to the Word of God with an open-hearted, receptive spirit of availability to be taught for a whole lifetime:

> But these are the ones sown on good ground, those who hear the word, accept it, and bear fruit: some thirtyfold, some sixty, and some a hundred (Mark 4:20).

Listen to His assuring promise: "some thirtyfold, some sixty, and some a hundred." They're all great measures of return, but they're more than a crop gathered in the autumn.

This is our Lord Jesus Himself talking about His truth manifesting in fruit in the issues of our human experience. It is God saying, "If you keep an openness to My Word, there will *always* be a fruitful harvest of that Word's promise and power in your life and circumstances!"

And, let no one make the mistake of thinking that 30-60-100 is a figure predestining some of us to a small measure and others to a greater one. The truth is, Jesus is pointing toward a promising increase! Read it this way, and you've caught the spirit of Jesus' words:

> This time you may only have a thirtyfold return, because your understanding and your response are limited. But if you keep an openness to My Word and My Spirit, you'll find a constant increasing as seed-sowing-cycles continue. Dear child, you're headed for an eventual hundred-fold increase of grace, purpose and blessing in your life!

The primary message is this: God's Word has been given to increase growth, fruitfulness and blessing—both in and through your life. And it is only as you and I remain open to it—teachable, shapable and responsive, *listening* with a heart ready to be taught and to obey—that fruit will appear and increase.

A FINAL NOTE

Finally, it's worth noting that every time the words "He who has ears to hear, let him hear" occur in the New Testament, Jesus is the one who is speaking. This is no casual expression, merely filling space like a human "Amen." Rather, it is the divine Son of God saying, "Don't ever close your ears or your heart to your need to be taught. It's the key to growth, to fruitfulness and to the joy of a multiplied harvest of God's blessing in your life."

His is the power. Ours may be the blessing.

How we listen will determine it all.

"LISTEN FOR THE WHISPERS"

It was the beloved Esther Kerr Rusthoi who coined that phrase, minting it in my consciousness in a priceless way several years ago. It was her way of exhorting believers to "hear what the Holy Spirit is saying to the Church"—or more specifically, to you.

To those who refuse to acknowledge a personal God, the suggestion that a loving Father speaks to His children is mocked as mere fantasy. To those ignorant of the Lord Jesus' constant ministry as Head of the Body of His Church, directing the activity of the members of that Body, such communication is considered unnecessary. To those who resist the tender voice of the Holy Spirit's prompting, impressing, balancing and prodding forward, such "whispers" are labeled fanaticism.

Eli's counsel to young Samuel is still practical wisdom to those who are just beginning to learn to hear the voice of God: "Say, 'Speak, LORD, for Your servant hears'" (1 Sam. 3:9).

Isaiah's prophecy forecasts a way of fruitfulness born from obedience: "Your ears shall hear a word behind you, saying, 'This is the way, walk in it'" (Isa. 30:21).

Jesus not only taught that sheep will know the Shepherd's voice, but He declared, "My sheep hear My voice . . . and they follow Me" (John 10:27). He asserted that receiving His Word—responding to it—is every bit as essential as recognizing it.

The kind of listening each of these passages describes is that which brings appropriate action. It is the simple and trusting response of a child, as in Samuel's case, or the sensitive and discerning response of a maturing learner, which Isaiah speaks about.

In describing the shepherd/sheep relationship as the basis for this order of hearing, He is saying (1) if you don't listen, you won't know where He's going, and (2) if you don't respond, you won't be very close to where He is.

In other words, everything is at stake: His guidance and His glory. Without listening carefully, we can miss both.

Friends, I hear a voice.

I think you do, too.

It sometimes calls, sometimes corrects, sometimes commands, sometimes directs, sometimes enthralls, sometimes teaches, sometimes demands and sometimes reaches . . .

. . . to touch the ear again with a loving, "Follow Me."

Listen.[3]

I take it that every Christian delivers himself up wholly to God in his baptism, when he renounces all the pomps and vanities of Satan, and enlists himself as a soldier to fight under Christ's banner all his life after.

DESIDERIUS ERASMUS, 1466-1536

PRINCIPLE

Jesus' command to all who receive His gift of life, the gift of salvation, is that they be baptized in water. This is a call not merely to observe a duty but, more importantly, to experience a dynamic. Obedience to this command means setting oneself on a riverlike pathway of submission to the lordship of Christ—a commitment to pursue discipleship as one dead to sin but alive to God through the power of the Holy Spirit (see Rom. 6:11).

PRACTICE

Having discovered the pivotal role water baptism fulfills in the believer's breaking through to a new and fulfilling lifestyle, I share the principles I have taught while witnessing more than 20,000 people baptized in water during the more than 30 years I pastored at The Church On The Way.

LIVING IN THE POWER OF BAPTISM

But Jesus answered and said to him, "Permit it to be so now, for thus it is fitting for us to fulfill all righteousness."

MATTHEW 3:15

The Spirit-filled life is not a mystical, unattainable lifestyle that God offers but keeps just out of our reach. It is a life of process—a life of becoming under the leadership of the Holy Spirit. As we have seen, the essence of discipleship is remaining shapable, teachable and flexible under our Lord Jesus Christ, who through His Spirit is in the business of building pillars.

So we need to deal with elements that are foundational, or fundamental, to our life in Christ and growth in Him. To do that we must give time to a consideration of the sacraments.

The idea behind what we call the sacraments is a striking one in the history of the Church. The word "sacrament" is derived from a Latin word that refers to an oath of allegiance. In Church terminology, it refers to the practice of a sacred ritual (for example, the Lord's Table) as a declaration that *trust* is being placed in the potential power of that exercise and that faith is being made manifest by the action taken.

Prior to Church usage, the idea of a sacrament involved a deposit that was made by two parties in a lawsuit. It was an action they established together in order to secure justice in a court of law in an attempt to receive a right, or claim. Similarly, the Church's concept of a sacrament proposes the participation of two parties: God (the party of the first part) has made a provision, and with specific actions, or deeds, we (the parties of the second part) respond to His provision. God, being the initiating party, has made a deposit of gracious provisions. For our part we, too, make a deposit: our faith to believe and our willing obedience to participate.

The two sacraments most common in the life of the Church are the sacraments of water baptism and the Lord's Table. Catholic Church tradition has observed as many as seven sacraments: baptism, confirmation, Eucharist, penance, holy orders, matrimony and anointing of the sick. In Protestant church tradition, these are not all observed. But for our study, I will only deal with the two sacraments almost all agree are biblically foundational to our walk with Christ: water baptism and the Lord's Table.

WATER BAPTISM

A solid grasp of water baptism is an essential part of cultivating the inner life. Whether or not you have already been baptized in water, I can think of several reasons why this discipline merits your attention and study.

First, our growth and depth of life as disciples of Christ depend on our moving beyond initiation experiences. Discipleship requires our seeing those truths and practices we've already obeyed (like water baptism) for *all* their implications. In other words, a disciple never simply experiences a truth or performs a sacrament, or act of faith, but he or she goes forth to *live out* that truth.

Second, we need to rethink the discipline of water baptism so we can sensibly and sensitively relay that truth to others. As disciples, we are given the opportunity to teach and influence new believers, so it is to their advantage and ours that we deepen our insights and understanding of the disciplines of the Spirit.

Third, it's possible that you, dear reader, have not yet been baptized. Through the years of my walk with Christ and as a leader, I have discovered a surprising number of believers—by no means a majority, but a substantial portion—who have walked with Christ for years, yet for one reason or another they have never been baptized in water. Because this is sometimes so, let me take a moment to address this issue. Whether it helps you or helps you help others, it's worth your time.

I've found that the primary reason many believers simply disregard baptism is they have somehow concluded that to be baptized is just a church tradition and so maybe it's only man's idea. Apparently, in too many churches water baptism is not being taught, either in the depth of its meaning or in the clarity of its biblical mandate by our Lord Jesus.

We all need to know that water baptism is a distinct biblical commandment—a personal responsibility, not simply a religious idea. And I don't mean "personal" as though it is ours to choose but rather personal in that Jesus has commanded it of *each one of us!*

> And He said to them, "Go into all the world and preach the gospel to every creature. He who believes and is baptized will be saved; but he who does not believe will be condemned" (Mark 16:15,16).

Hear it? Baptism is as important as the Great Commission. Jesus told His disciples to go to the world, preach the gospel and "make disciples of all the nations, baptizing them in the name of the Father and of the Son and of the Holy Spirit" (Matt. 28:19). Baptism is a straightforward matter of obedi-ence to Christ.

Some people don't take the step to be baptized in water because they have experienced baptism in the Holy Spirit *first,* and they suppose somehow that baptism in water isn't necessary.

But the Bible shows quite the opposite. Look at Acts 10:44-48:

> While Peter was still speaking these words, the Holy
> Spirit fell upon all those who heard the word. And those
> of the circumcision who believed were astonished, as
> many as came with Peter, because the gift of the Holy
> Spirit had been poured out on the Gentiles also. For they
> heard them speak with tongues and magnify God. Then
> Peter answered, "Can anyone forbid water, that these
> should not be baptized who have received the Holy
> Spirit just as we have?" And he commanded them to be
> baptized in the name of the Lord.

Though the group at the house of Cornelius had been filled with
the Holy Spirit, Peter still directed that they be baptized in water.
There's no way around it. *No* experience, however grand and glorious, is a substitute for water baptism.

Others believe in baptism but have not accepted the discipline
for themselves. They have their reasons. For example, I've encountered a surprising number of dear believers who haven't been baptized because the thought of being immersed beneath the water is
tormentingly frightening to them. Someone may think this exaggerated or ridiculous, but such fears are real. However loving, sympathetic and understanding we should be, this reluctance still
must be confronted. And I'm thrilled to report that in many such
cases, when we have together bound and overruled the spirit of
fear in Jesus' name and with biblical authority, we have seen great
deliverances occur as the individual obeyed and was baptized.
Obedience is followed by deliverance! Hallelujah!

Some baptismal candidates I've known avoided baptism
because of fear of embarrassment; they were concerned about
"looking funny all wet." This obviously must be confronted gra-

ciously as well. While the Bible doesn't mandate that observers be present at baptism, there usually are—and it's desirable. Baptism is one of life's greatest opportunities to be a witness! Let's capitalize on it. Invite friends to this occasion, and let's make this triumphant moment *count!* And if there is still a lurking concern that perhaps he or she may not appear all that neat when he or she comes up out of the water, hair streaming in every direction, it's good to obey simply to overcome pride. It's always wise for a disciple to challenge *any* preoccupation with "how good I look." Obedience to our Savior and Master is the ultimate consideration at all points of our lives, and all other concerns must bow before Him.

As a disciple, such thoughtfulness can enhance your ability to assist others. Strange or simple as such objections may seem, they are issues I've needed to address with individuals in order to assure their personal obedience to baptism.

Fourth, you may be considering the idea of being baptized *again.* Of course, there are various Christian traditions concerning baptism, both in the *form* of baptism as well as the *timing.* Perhaps you were baptized as an infant at the wish of your parents, so you are wondering whether you need to be baptized again by your own choice as an adult.

Or perhaps you were baptized earlier in your Christian life, but in the intervening time you have wandered from a close walk with God. Now, having returned to the Lord, you may wonder, *Should I be baptized again?* The central issue, dear friend, is that you *be* baptized!

A number of times I have been asked, "Since I was baptized as an infant (or as a child) and I didn't really know what I was doing, would it be irreverent for me to be baptized again?" I hasten to reply, "Never!" How could it *possibly* be irreverent to *now* confirm, by your own decision, what was volunteered for you by parents who earlier desired that you make a commitment to the Lord? That's how I have answered that question for years, without *demanding* a rebaptism.

But I have found that the reason people ask this question is usually because the Holy Spirit is dealing with their hearts. And if He does, they ought never to feel hesitant or guilty. Listen: You are not violating the love and care that was shown by parents (or other authorities in your life) who requested that you be baptized when you were younger. Rebaptism is not a rejection of parental love!

Likewise, if you were baptized earlier in your walk with Christ and then for a season distanced yourself from Him through disobedience, but now feel prompted to be rebaptized, you are *not* negating the reality of your earlier walk or salvation experience. The act of baptism in water is to be monitored by your heart's obedience to the Holy Spirit and not by undue fear or reverence for the past. The issue is to obey the Lord of your life! Be baptized.

DEPTH OF MEANING

Now let's examine the depth in the meaning of this fundamental discipline. Though we have been baptized, fully acknowledging its importance, we're still called to *abide* in the truths baptism expresses. So how can we live more fully in the power of those principles as Jesus' disciples? What does it mean to live the baptized life?

Baptism and Obedience

To live the baptized life is to live in an abiding recollection of my baptism with this mind-set: *I have submitted myself in obedience to*

Jesus' lordship, and this is my lifetime commitment. My will is to do His will. Jesus Himself identified this as a fundamental issue in water baptism (see Matt. 3:14,15).

Baptism and the Fullness of the Holy Spirit

To live the baptized life is to be open to the fullness of the Holy Spirit. Peter tells of the promise awaiting us when we come to the waters of baptism. "Repent, and let every one of you be baptized," he says. And then he adds glorious words of promise, "and you shall receive the gift of the Holy Spirit" (Acts 2:38).

Hear these words—*now!*

Hardly a week goes by at The Church On The Way when we don't witness people who, *as they come up from the waters of baptism,* are at the same time filled—right there—with the Holy Spirit. They begin to worship the Lord supernaturally by the power of the Holy Spirit! Peter's words point toward that possibility.

Baptism and the Death of the Old Man

The apostle Paul reveals another aspect of baptismal truth:

> Or do you not know that as many of us as were baptized into Christ Jesus were baptized into His death? Therefore we were buried with Him through baptism into death, that just as Christ was raised from the dead by the glory of the Father, even so we also should walk in newness of life (Rom. 6:3,4).

Notice how the truth of baptism's significance continues to expand. Paul shows baptism not only as an act of obedience and an opening of Holy Spirit fullness, but also as an action of

As strangers and pilgrims that are baptized into the resurrection of Jesus Christ . . . [we] are to follow Him in a wise and heavenly course of life, in the mortification of the worldly desires, and in purifying and preparing [our] souls for the blessed enjoyment of God.

WILLIAM LAW
1686-1761

commitment to *burial*. Like a funeral at sea, we are to bury our old ways in the waters where Jesus has called us to meet Him. It's a real "commitment," if you will. We use the word "commit" at funerals as the casket is lowered into the ground. Similarly, my commitment to Jesus Christ is manifest in my willingness to say, "For all the remaining years of my life, I shall be dead to my past and my old carnal ways."

But that's not the end of it. For while I'm dying to my old self, I am also making another Bible-taught announcement. Just as I am buried—immersed in the water—I also *rise again!* As I come up out of the water, I am declaring, "From now on I will draw on the power of the resurrection life of my Lord Jesus!" Just as He was buried, so we have been buried with Him; just as He arose, so we have risen in the newness of His life and the power of His Spirit.

But if the Spirit of Him who raised Jesus from the dead dwells in you,

He who raised Christ from the dead will also give life to your mortal bodies through His Spirit who dwells in you (Rom. 8:11).

To live the baptized life means allowing the life-giving Spirit of God to resurrect you on a daily basis, *lifting* you above the dead habits of the past and into newness of life for today and tomorrow.

Baptism and Circumcision of the Heart

The Word calls to mind yet another ritual to expand our understanding of water baptism:

> In Him you were also circumcised with the circumcision made without hands, by putting off the body of the sins of the flesh, by the circumcision of Christ, buried with Him in baptism, in which you also were raised with Him through faith in the working of God, who raised Him from the dead (Col. 2:11,12).

Linking it to the picture of our death, burial and resurrection into the newness of life in Christ, God's Word presents the figure of the Old Testament rite of circumcision. Of course, that ancient rite involved the removal of the foreskin of the male sex organ, but the physical nature of the practice should not distract us from the dynamic symbolism applicable today. We need to capture this, because a brief moment of insight into the implications of baptism as circumcision can reveal a very powerful but practical truth. In the delicacy of the literal physiology of circumcision involving that most private part of the body, there are important spiritual lessons to be learned.

In baptism God wants to cut away flesh. That is, He wants to remove carnality from our lives—things that are superfluous to the needs for which He has created us. Understand this: Just as the removal of that small portion of excess flesh from the physical organ of the body does not reduce or inhibit the capacity of that part of the body, there are excessive aspects of our behavior that God may want to remove from our lives. This removal will not inhibit our capacity for good things in His order, but it will remove unnecessary things that are outside His purposes and design.

By way of illustration, notice that it was not until *after* Abraham was circumcised that the miracle of Isaac's conception and birth happened! I have often wondered, *How many people never experience the release or fulfillment of God's promises because they have not been baptized in submission to the Lord?* To live the baptized life means to be fully obedient and open to the Spirit of promise and to possibilities yet to be born in our lives. For Abraham, reproductivity in God's realm of promise didn't happen until after his circumcision. Similarly, there may be realms of fruit-bearing capacity in many lives that are only waiting their obedience to Jesus—to circumcision via the waters of baptism.

You see, baptism is not a ritual to be performed but rather a dynamic to be experienced! The analogy of circumcision makes it clear that baptism is a time when God cuts away "flesh" as we come under His order and releases power to bring about His promised life and purpose through us. Just as circumcision dealt with a private part, so these things happen in the privacy of our hearts as our Lord works His will and power in us.

Baptism and Deliverance

Add to this one last illustration regarding baptism:

> Moreover, brethren, I do not want you to be unaware that all our fathers were under the cloud, all passed through

the sea, all were *baptized* into Moses in the cloud and in
the sea (1 Cor. 10:1,2, emphasis added).

Here's a marvelous picture of Israel's coming out of Egypt, history's most dramatic deliverance from slavery unto destiny! See
how the children of Israel "all were baptized into Moses in the
cloud and in the sea." The Bible uses the miraculous moment of
the sea's parting to give us dynamic insight into the kind of
blessing God is ready to impart at *our* water baptism.

See the picture: Moments before, the Israelites had their
backs to the wall, but now they have come through a pathway of
deliverance. Can you imagine their joy? The oppressors who had
enslaved them for four centuries were vanquished as the waters
of the Red Sea swallowed them.

Listen, loved one. *Water baptism is intended to be a moment of
deliverance for us, too.*

Things to which we've been enslaved, the fetters by which
we've been shackled, the snares in which we've been entangled
through actions of our adversary—when deliverance is needed
from hellish oppression, *all are broken!*

Water baptism is *not* just a church tradition. It is a miracle
moment!

In it I obey the lordship of Jesus. In it I welcome the Holy
Spirit. In it I bury my past. In it my heart is circumcised so new
life power and God's fullest promise for my life might be realized. In it every bondage and every yoke is broken, and my future
is opened to fullest freedom in Christ that I may arise and walk
in the life-giving power of my living Savior.

These are the dynamic principles demonstrated in water
baptism. Each is a present reality awaiting the disciple's obedience. So, come—whether you've been baptized or not—come and
possess the promise.

Be baptized. *Live* baptized.

Pray with me:

Jesus, today I want the power potential for a baptized person to be mine. I want to walk in openness to Your Spirit, dead to my past, circumcised from unproductivity so fruitfulness might abound, and freed from every bond and yoke of the adversary.

The Heavens Opened

Remember what happened at the waters of baptism when Jesus experienced this moment:

Then Jesus, when He had been baptized, came up immediately from the water; and behold, the heavens were opened to Him, and He saw the Spirit of God descending like a dove and alighting upon Him. And suddenly a voice came from heaven, saying, "This is My beloved Son, in whom I am well pleased" (Matt. 3:16,17).

When the sinless Son of God submitted to be baptized, *the heavens opened* to Him, *the Spirit descended* upon Him and *the Father spoke* from heaven. And these blessings also await the believer who will follow Jesus in baptism.

"The heavens were opened" doesn't mean there was a crack in the sky and Jesus saw something of the eternal city in the distance. Rather, it means that the realm of invisible reality became perceptible—the spiritual realm became a functional, perceived arena of impending action.

The Lord wants the same for us: an entrance into a realm of relationship with Him where the invisible is not mysterious but, instead, is perceived as an arena in which we function with confidence. God makes us disciples who, seeing the invisible not as bizarre but as a real dimension of life, are as comfortable relating to things of the Spirit as we are operating in the physical realm.

Just as Jesus entered this dimension—from that time onward warring against the devil, casting out demons and insightfully looking into human need—so He invites us to the same way of life. The Lord wants us to be baptized into a practical relationship of insight and godly perspective in the spiritual issues of life.

Just as the Holy Spirit came upon our Lord and (as we have already observed) the fullness of the Holy Spirit is made available to us, let us remember that *living* the baptized life means *abiding* in that fullness.

And what of the Father's approval? When He said, "This is My Son, in whom I am well pleased," was this important to Jesus? Why would the Father have spoken those words if they were not expressing something that would be confirming and affirming to His own Son? I suppose someone might object, "There is *no way* Jesus needed to be affirmed!" But wait, dear friend, don't overlook the reality of His humanity. He came to us as a man, taking on the same feelings that we have; and even though He lived in absolute sinlessness, He also knew what it meant to desire a Father's approval.

You and I do, too.

And as you and I accept the discipline of baptism—both by being baptized and living as one baptized—the same joyous realization will be ours as well. It's the portion of obedient sons and daughters, and you will sense it as His words resound in your soul: *I'm pleased with you.*

When Christ calls a man, He bids him come and die. It may be a death like that of the first disciples who had to leave home and work to follow Him, or it may be a death like Luther's, who had to leave the monastery and go out into the world. But it is the same death every time—death in Jesus Christ, the death of the old man at His call. . . . In fact, every command of Jesus is a call to die, with all our affections and lusts. But we do not want to die, and therefore Jesus Christ and His call are necessarily our death and our life.

DIETRICH BONHOEFFER, 1906-1945

PRINCIPLE

The observance of the Lord's Table is a practice that frames the centerpiece of Christian faith, the Cross, and a practice that focuses on the central person of our worship, Jesus our Savior. To participate in Communion with understanding is to transcend mere tradition, for this is where the living Word and living worship converge to release the power of Christ's presence at His Table.

PRACTICE

First, we will look at the dangers of either a merely ritual observance or a casual neglect of Communion. We will then examine five primary dynamics available through vital partaking of, or living participation in, the Lord's Table.

CELEBRATING THE LORD'S TABLE

Take, eat; this is My body. . . . Drink . . . all of you.

MATTHEW 26:26,27

As with water baptism, the Lord's Table is a practice that Jesus established, directing us to do this in remembrance of Him:

> For I received from the Lord that which I also delivered to you: that the Lord Jesus on the same night in which He was betrayed took bread; and when He had given thanks, He broke it and said, "Take, eat; this is My body which is broken for you; do this in remembrance of Me." In the same manner He also took the cup after supper, saying "This cup is the new covenant in My blood. This do, as often as you drink it, in remembrance of Me." For as often as you eat this bread and drink this cup, you proclaim the Lord's death till He comes (1 Cor. 11:23-26).

He established no calendar for this practice. He simply said, "As often as you do it, remember Me." I have friends who partake of the Lord's Table daily as a part of their private devotions. Other traditions only observe it once a year—usually on Good Friday or on the occasion of the Hebrew Passover. And some Christians observe the Lord's Table (also called Communion, Eucharist or Mass) every week. Our church partakes the first Sunday of every month and on a few special seasonal occasions throughout the year.

While Jesus did not give specific direction as to frequency, He did say that He wanted His people to return *regularly* to the fountainhead of life—to the Cross and His victory there. Why?

REMEMBERING TO REMEMBER

One well-known entertainer, who happens to be a member of the congregation I have served, learned at least one reason why. It happened this way.

By reason of his many travels and irregular schedule, this man is often away on Sunday. But when he is home during the week, I might say to his credit, he will be present at the midweek service. He is committed to assembling with other believers, as well as ministering to those with whom he fellowships.

One Sunday he commented, "I was so glad to be here for the Lord's Table." He said, "You know, Jack, I recently went through a time of real affliction, when suddenly I realized it had been five months since I had been present at church on the first Sunday when we observe the Lord's Table."

That morning he received nourishment and strength, both spiritually and physically. He went on to testify to his sense of dynamic spiritual renewal centering on the refreshing which came to his whole being as a result of celebrating Communion. There were very few calories in the small portion that was served. But the power and benefit available at the Table do not come from human nutrients; they come from divine sustenance promised to us in the Word of God.

When Jesus said, "Do this in remembrance of Me," He was not calling us to *commiserate* over either His suffering or our sin. He was calling us to *commemorate* His announcement: "It is finished!" (John 19:30). And with our celebration of His triumph over all sin, death and hell, He would call our attention to this reminder: "This is for you, and it's for you today." Never forget it! Regularly come back to the Cross, and rejoice in and freshly receive Christ's victory!

Communion is a good way to begin any new season of your life. Periodically participate in the Lord's Table in your home, with members of your family. You could lead it or invite others to participate in its presentation. Of course, this is not to suggest nonattendance at church or render as unnecessary the pastoral-elder ministry of the church. But let home celebrations of the Lord's Table *complement* the regular practice in our churches, doing this not as a substitute for Body life but rather as a means to apply the power of the sacrament in our homes.

With what understanding ought we to approach the Lord's Table, whether at church or at home? Let us consider this sacrament and its beauty as well as its dynamic in our lives.

IT'S A CELEBRATION OF VICTORY

Revelation 12:11 says, "And they overcame him by the blood of the Lamb and by the word of their testimony, and they did not love their lives to the death." This proclamation notes a dominion that is assured to the Church. We will triumph over the powers of darkness in the last days' struggle, and victory is linked to the abiding testimony of the blood of Jesus.

Every time I take the cup of the Lord's Table in my hands, I am reminded it is intended to be the celebration of not only the victory *won* but also a victory now available. The victory that was accomplished with Jesus' words "It is finished!" means that our salvation is complete, our sins are forgiven and we are justified by His death. It's a declaration Jesus wants us never to forget, and that victory applies to every confrontation with flesh or devil we may face today. Knowing that we *have* and *will* overcome by the blood of the Lamb, we should carry that understanding to the Lord's Table and give thanks.

The meaning of the word *eucharisteo* (the Greek verb from which "Eucharist" is derived) is "I thank." It's the central focus of our response, to be praiseful in a tone of victory. As we gather in celebration at the Lord's Table, the quality of our praise and thanks should be proportionate to Calvary's victory. The atmosphere of remembrance at the Lord's Table is to be one of feasting and celebrating—that's the reverent and praiseful style appropriate in the light of "It is finished!"

IT'S A PROCLAMATION OF REDEMPTION

For as often as you eat this bread and drink this cup, you proclaim the Lord's death till He comes (1 Cor. 11:26).

I will not drink of this fruit of the vine from now on until that day when I drink it new with you in My Father's kingdom (Matt. 26:29).

The Lord's Table proclaims not only the redemption that's been accomplished, but also the redemption we *anticipate* at His return! It was Jesus' command that when we begin to see certain things coming to pass in our world, very much as they are now, that we lift up our heads, because our redemption draws near (see Luke 21:28).

In this spirit, the Bible says that every time you and I partake of the Lord's cup, we're making a *preachment* (the word "proclaim" could be translated literally that way). Ours is a message of a Savior who not only is coming again but who right now is available to save all who will receive the good news of His death, resurrection and salvation.

When we make the proclamation of redemption around the Lord's Table, we are sharing the redemption He's given. "Communion" is derived from the word, *koinonia,* which emphasizes that in celebrating Communion we are mutually sharing in a quality of redemptive life which was secured at the Cross. In 1 Corinthians 10:16, Paul said, "The cup of blessing which we bless, is it not the communion of the blood of Christ? The bread which we break, is it not the communion of the body of Christ?" Our present victory over the powers of darkness—our anticipation of the joy of His coming—should bring high praise for such redemptive glory!

I hope this doesn't seem irreverent to anyone, but when I think about all of this—redemption past, present and to come—I want to take the cup of the Lord's Table and say, "Jesus, I'll drink to that! Hallelujah!" This is the spirit of faith, celebration and proclamation He wants us to experience together with Him at His Table.

It's a Declaration of Dependence

Matthew, Mark and Luke connect their teaching on the Lord's Table to the Last Supper, the meal Jesus shared with His disciples on the night before He was crucified. John offers a parallel teaching that is connected to an earlier season of Jesus' ministry in Galilee, after He fed the 5,000 and then met inquiries at another location. As the people congregated, hoping for another feast,

Faithful cross! above all other, one and only noble tree! None in foliage, none in blossom, none in fruit thy peer may be: Sweetest wood and sweetest iron! Sweetest weight is hung on thee.

VENANTIUS
HONORIUS
FORTUNATUS
540-600(?)

He said to them, "You're not coming because you want what I have to minister. You're coming because you saw a miracle that filled your stomachs" (see John 6:26).

He challenged the multitude with the issue of discipleship, beginning with an analogy that became so vivid that it puzzled many onlookers. Here's what He said: "You have to eat My body and drink My blood or you'll have no life in you" (see John 6:53). Much of the crowd left then, for it sounded to them as though He were introducing some bizarre form of ritual cannibalism.

Jesus didn't bother to correct those who simply wanted "miracle loaves," but His words sought to comb the crowd to find those willing to learn and enjoy a real relationship with Him. When so many of the people had left, His disciples said, "Lord, this is a very hard thing You've said" (see v. 60). He answered, "Listen to the words that I'm speaking. They are spirit, and they are life" (see v. 63).

Listen again. Do you hear Him? He's saying, "I'm speaking of a *spiritual* truth. You *do* need to drink My blood in its *spiritual* power. You *do* need to eat My body for its *spiritual* nourishment!"

A person who is seriously anemic may need periodic blood transfusions to regain or retain strength and health. Similarly, by partaking of the Lord's Table, we receive transfusions of His holy power through the pure dynamic of the blood of Jesus Christ—power to conquer sin in any way it seeks to dominate our lives.

The Israelites' deliverance from Egypt is another illustration of the dynamics of the Lord's Table. The Hebrews placed the blood of a lamb on their doorways prior to the move of God that would finally cause their deliverance, but then they ate the flesh of the sacrifice in order to gain strength for the coming journey. So when the Lamb of God says, "Come and remember Me and take of My body," He is saying, "Be nourished and be strengthened for the journey ahead." As people who, like Israel, are being delivered (see 2 Cor. 1:10), we need strength for the road. Therefore, we come to the Lord's Table in acknowledged dependence, to draw on God-ordained resources in Christ.

IT'S A TIME FOR SELF-EXAMINATION

In 1 Corinthians 11:27-31, the apostle Paul underscores this need:

Whoever eats this bread or drinks this cup of the Lord in an unworthy manner will be guilty of the body and blood of the Lord. But let a man examine himself, and so let him eat of that bread and drink of that cup. For he who eats and drinks in an unworthy manner eats and drinks judgment to himself, not discerning the Lord's body. For this reason many are weak and sick among you, and many sleep. For if we would judge ourselves, we would not be judged.

Dokimazo ("examine") is the Greek verb used (v. 28), a word descriptive of running a test. In other words, the Word says, at the Lord's Table, test your own heart toward the Lord and toward one another. What are your attitudes?

Earlier in this same letter to the church at Corinth, Paul indicated he was troubled about people within the congregation quarreling with one another (see 1 Cor. 1:10,11). He was concerned about people who were living with a reckless or indifferent attitude toward the sin of division and of lovelessness. In the scripture above about self-examination, the truth resounds in such a way that we might apply Paul's appeal this way: When you come to the Table, take the occasion to examine yourself to see if there's division between you and other members of the congregation. You can't partake of the Lord's body when your heart is divided toward others in the local church body, for whom Jesus allowed Himself to be broken! Don't come to the Table with such division or a passive attitude toward this or any other sin. It's *this very exercise* that commemorates Jesus' death for your sins, so receive His enablement to be free from them.

Hear it, loved one. Communion—the sacrament of the Lord's Supper—is a time to examine our relationship with God and our relationship with one another. We're coming to the Table of forgiveness, so we cannot be unforgiving. We're coming to the Table of cleansing, so we must confess uncleanness in ourselves.

The significance of this heart preparation at the Lord's Table is distinctly important, but there's another side of the "examine yourselves" truth that has been sorely distorted.

Have you ever heard it suggested that you ought not come to the Lord's Table because you've stumbled, or sinned, during the past week or month? In other words, if you've failed the Lord of recent date, you had perhaps better consider whether or not it's safe for you to come to the Lord's Table.

Such a warning is usually argued on the basis of verses 29,30: "[They partook] in an unworthy manner. . . . For this reason many are weak and sick among you, and many sleep." Misinterpretation has led some to suggest that God struck these people dead—that "unworthy" partaking was the action of believers who came to the Lord's Table despite having recently sinned in some way, thereby invoking God's judgment on them.

Where such teaching prevails, fear and intimidation follow.

Worse, there are circles of Christian Communion where the Lord's Table is used as a disciplinary device. For example: "Because you have failed, we won't let you observe Communion for three months (or six months or a year) until you verify your holiness."

Now, it's not my place to administrate other groups' traditions, but it is my business to handle the Word of God. So I want to challenge such abuse of the truth.

Nowhere does the Word of God give the directive that denied access to the Communion table is a means for applying corrective discipline. To say to the person "You can't come to the Lord's Table because you've sinned" is equivalent to saying to a starving man, "You can't eat any food until you get over your malnutrition." It's a ridiculous and counterproductive proposition!

We are called to come to *His* Table—not man's—to receive forgiveness for our failures. We are called to come to *His* Table to receive nourishment and power for practical living in Christ! And because it's *His* Table, His Word should govern who is allowed and who isn't. Jesus says:

Come to Me, all you who labor and are heavy laden, and
I will give you rest (Matt. 11:28).

All that the Father gives Me will come to Me, and the one
who comes to Me I will by no means cast out (John 6:37).

It's a Provision of Healing

If to partake in an unworthy manner does *not* mean we are to
reflect on our unworthiness, what do these words in 1 Corinthians
11:29 mean?

First, let's settle an essential proposition. If the question has
to do with your or my worthiness, then there *isn't* any question!
We *are* unworthy. Always. None of us has ever been worthy of
anything God has ever done for us!

The answer is in seeing the meaning of "worthy" as it occurs
in this passage. The word translated "worthy" *(axios)* draws on
the concept of worthiness as it had to do with weight, not perfection. For example, in ancient times, the actual weight of a
coin is what gave the coin its value, or worth. Through frequent
usage coins would lose small amounts of their weight and thus
they became reduced in value, or buying power.

Now in this light, we can see that in this passage the apostle
Paul is saying, "When you come to the Lord's Table, bring *the full
weight of your understanding and faith*." Come to this moment recognizing the full weight and full worth of what Christ has done
for you at Calvary. Come and partake of full forgiveness, full
deliverance and full healing!

The Word not only tells us Jesus' blood was shed for our sins,
but also that His body was broken for our suffering and our
afflictions. The Bible says, "He Himself took our infirmities and
bore our sicknesses" (Matt. 8:17). So we can see that healing is

available to us, bequeathed among the many resources available to us through His cross.

Now it becomes clear why Paul reflects on those who had come to the Table unworthily (i.e., without drawing on the full weight of resources available) and says, "For this reason, many are weak and sick." Paul is *not* pointing out their lack of perfection but rather their need for *participation*—for fully partaking in faith and receiving *all* Jesus has for them at His table.

So, as His disciples, let us regularly enter into

the celebration of victory,

the proclamation of redemption,

the declaration of dependence,

the examination of ourselves

and the provision of healing.

Invite the Holy Spirit to anoint your time of participation in this holy sacrament, so you may benefit *fully*. His table is the central focus of our worship and the central resource for our walk in faith. The growing disciple will find he or she needs not only the spiritual nutrition afforded here, but also the health, correction and release from affliction that the sacrament of Communion is intended to provide.

ALL IS WELL

Raised by hate upon a hill, stark there stands a cross of wood,
Look, the Man they take and kill is the Lamb, the Son of God.
See the blood now freely flow; "It is finished," hear Him cry!
Who can understand or know: Death has won; yet death will die.
All is well, all is well,
Through Christ, our Conq'rer,
All is well.
All is well, all is well,

Through Christ, our Conq'rer,
All is well.
Slashing wounds now scar the Lamb,
Blemish free until He's slain,
Hammer blows into His hand thunder forth again, again.
See His Body raised in scorn, see the spear now split His side!
Yet the vict'ry shall be won by this Man thus crucified.
Look! The Cross now raised on high—
Symbol of Christ's reign above.
Cow'ring demons fear and fly, driv'n before the flame of love.
All of hell is mystified; Satan thought this hour his gain.
See God's wisdom glorified: death destroyed in Jesus' name.
Here is hope in hopelessness, here is joy where all is pain.
Here a fount of righteousness flows to all who make their claim.
Come and drink here, come and live.
Come and feast on life and peace.
In the Cross God's all He gives, in the Cross is full release.
Tow'ring o'er all history stands the Cross of Christ the King.
Crossroad of all destiny, at the Cross is ev'rything.
See here death hung on a Cross, see self slain upon a tree,
See disease and ev'ry loss overthrown through Calvary!
All is well, all is well,
Through Christ, our Conq'rer,
All is well.
All is well, all is well,
Through Christ, our Conq'rer,
All is well.

J.W.H.

To be a Christian means to forgive the inexcusable, because God has forgiven the inexcusable in you. This is hard. It is perhaps not so hard to forgive a single injury. But to forgive the incessant provocations of daily life—to keep on forgiving the bossy mother-in-law, the bullying husband, the nagging wife, the selfish daughter, the deceitful so—how can we do it? Only, I think, by remembering where we stand, by meaning our words when we say in our prayers each night, "Forgive us our trespasses as we forgive those who trespass against us." We are offered forgiveness on no other terms. To refuse it means to refuse God's mercy for ourselves.

C. S. LEWIS, 1989-1963

———∞———

PRINCIPLE

The forgiveness of sin given freely to us in Christ, through His atoning death and justifying work, opens a fountainhead of grace that flows to us without measure. That graciousness is a summons to every believer, saying, "Freely you have received, so freely give"—a call which cannot remain unanswered except at the expense of blockage, bondage and withering of the soul.

———∞———

PRACTICE

I offer a confession of my embarrassing self-discovery, at the hands of the Holy Spirit, of the smallness of my own soul seen in my unperceived yet real unforgiveness toward a guy named Joe. In the context of my awakening to righteousness, I share the insights I gained into Jesus' great story lesson on the unforgiving servant found in Matthew 18.

WALKING IN THE SPIRIT OF FORGIVENESS

I forgave you all that debt because you begged me. Should you not also have had compassion on your fellow servant, just as I had pity on you?

MATTHEW 18:32,33

If any single truth has become dominative in my understanding of Christian living, it's the breadth of the implications Jesus teaches regarding forgiveness. Before reading the story He told to make His point, let me tell a personal story of my own that describes how He helped me understand *His*.

Shortly after Anna and I were married, we visited the Nebraska plains where she had been raised as the near youngest of nine children. It was an initiating trip for me, as I hadn't yet met most of her family. That's when I met Joe.

I was so warmly received by almost everyone that it was a little surprising when Joe responded differently. I sensed a low-grade rejection, but I took it in stride, for I understood Joe's aloofness. I recognized that it was related to his spiritual condition.

Joe was away from God.

Even though he had been raised in the things of the Lord, Joe had developed a way of distancing himself from anyone whom he felt might possibly crowd his lifestyle. Understanding this, I purposely did nothing to make him feel as though I were on a crusade for his soul. Instead, I went out of my way to be friendly, to treat him as a brother—one I would accept and trust, no matter what he chose to do.

Obviously, I wanted to see Joe return to a walk with Christ. But even though I was his relative in training for the ministry, I avoided doing any offensive "religious things" that might drive him further from the Lord. I didn't try to slip spiritual messages into the conversation or push an agenda when we were together. I just tried to be a friend.

It didn't work.

Although there was no apparent reason for Joe to be less than brotherly to me, although I tried to be sensitive and winsome, Joe wouldn't crack—not even slightly. He withdrew from even my warmest of overtures. I thought his coolness would wear away with time, but it didn't. Over the years he maintained a distinct relational distance, and eventually, I lost patience.

The turning point came 15 years into my acquaintance with Joe. It wasn't good.

TIRED OF TRYING

Anna, the kids and I made a trip back to Nebraska to celebrate her folks' 50th wedding anniversary. The celebration was marvelously heartwarming, with friends and family gathered from all points of the compass. And that's the mood and setting that turned out so badly—at least it was bad for me.

I was in the backyard talking to Joe one day. And as we conversed, his studied reserve started to rankle me. Although I didn't recognize it, I was on a headlong path to hardheartedness. We had been relatives for years and talked together many times, but on this day my frustration with his chilling treatment—an almost snobbish air of rejection—reached a breaking point. Something unobservable to the eye yet very real in the soul snapped inside me. I was closing the door—a private, unspoken decision resulting from years of mounting fatigue and impatience with Joe's attitude. I was through trying.

I had never felt this way toward anyone, but neither had I ever felt this shut out by anyone. I knew it wasn't paranoia on my part, because I felt no such rejection from anyone else. He had continually demonstrated personal resistance to common decency, and I was about to silently retaliate in kind. I remember the decisive moment well. I simply but angrily thought to myself, *I'm through!*

That was it. I was simply tired of trying.

I didn't physically turn my back and walk away from him at that moment; but in my heart and attitude toward Joe, I did. I was washing my hands of him, done trying to be his friend. I wouldn't realize it until later, but Joe had become a victim of my unforgiveness.

STABBED TO AWARENESS

Summer and autumn passed that year, and soon it was Valentine's Day. I'll never forget that overcast morning at home in California when God stabbed me with the truth. Until then I had been entirely oblivious to my failure, for I felt entirely justified in my decision to be as indifferent to my relationship with Joe as he obviously was. He was far from my mind and heart that morning—very far. I hadn't thought about that summertime decision since the moment it occurred, but it was all about to come crashing down around my head in a wave of spiritual understanding.

As I strolled into the kitchen, my eye was caught by a Valentine card lying on the table. I flipped it open, having read the front, which was a setup—a humorous preview to what I knew would be a funny punchline. But the joke turned out to be on me.

While I can't remember the punchline printed in the card, I will never forget the handwritten words at the bottom. They were from Joe's teenage daughter, who had sent the card to my daughter. The two girls had struck up an ongoing friendship, and they were growing up together half a continent apart. The card was simply part of their continuing correspondence. But it was also an ice pick in God's hands that He would use to shatter my frozen heart. The note at the bottom read: "Dear Becki, I just wanted to add a note to thank you for mentioning in your last letter that you are regularly praying for my dad to come back to Jesus."

In that moment the Holy Spirit jabbed me awake to two things. First, He exposed the unworthiness of my counter-rejection attitude toward Joe. He had used my daughter to jar me to an awareness that two teenagers were exchanging mutual concern and sharing prayers for a man I had the unholy, blinded audacity to give up on. Worse, I awakened to a second humbling fact.

Don't ask me to try to explain why, because I *did* care about Joe's soul and I *was* pursuing faithful ministry all the time I had known him. But the awful truth is that in the 15 years I had known Joe, I could not remember even *once* specifically praying for him!

Go ahead, fire the questions: *Why,* Jack? You never prayed for him *once,* even *before* that summer? The only answer I can give is yes. I cared. But apparently my attitude was so hardened by his rejection that it had blinded me, blocking my recognition of my own neglect.

Still, there was another dynamic at work that Valentine morning. In mercy, the Spirit of God was birthing repentance in my heart—and love.

I literally fell to my knees alone there in the kitchen, and I began to weep. I repented for my blindness, for my hard-heartedness, for my impatience, for my writing off Joe. And I asked God's forgiveness for the prayerlessness that my unperceived as well as known attitudes had begotten in me.

Then I prayed for Joe. I prayed with an entirely new sense of love—for the man, for his soul, for Joe. "No matter how he is, I *care*, Lord!" And I truly did.

That experience was one of my life's greatest lessons, for it set me on a path that led to a new understanding of the power of a spirit of forgiveness—remembering how much more God's mercy has been shown to me than I'll *ever* need to show someone else. A spirit of forgiveness is a fundamental requirement for every disciple's life and learning.

Jesus gave a lengthy story to illustrate this, showing both the need for our learning this spirit and the dangers if we don't. So before I tell you the rest of my story about Joe, take a look with me at Jesus' parable. It's a long passage and possibly so well known you might think you know it better than you do. So read it slowly, please, perhaps even penciling in an underscoring of key points you notice.

JESUS' LESSON ON FORGIVENESS

Then Peter came to Him and said, "Lord, how often shall my brother sin against me, and I forgive him? Up to seven times?"

Jesus said to him, "I do not say to you, up to seven times, but up to seventy times seven. Therefore the kingdom of heaven is like a certain king who wanted to settle accounts with his servants. And when he had begun to settle accounts, one was brought to him who owed him ten thousand talents. But as he was not able to pay, his master commanded that he be sold, with his wife and children and all that he had, and that payment be made.

"The servant therefore fell down before him, saying, 'Master, have patience with me, and I will pay you all.' Then the master of that servant was moved with compassion, released him, and forgave him the debt.

"But that servant went out and found one of his fellow servants who owed him a hundred denarii; and he laid hands on him and took him by the throat, saying, 'Pay me what you owe!'

"So his fellow servant fell down at his feet and begged him, saying, 'Have patience with me, and I will pay you all.' And he would not, but went and threw him into prison till he should pay the debt. So when his fellow servants saw what had been done, they were very grieved, and came and told their master all that had been done.

"Then his master, after he had called him, said to him, 'You wicked servant! I forgave you all that debt because you begged me. Should you not also have had compassion on your fellow servant, just as I had pity on you?' And his master was angry, and delivered him to the torturers until he should pay all that was due to him.

"So My heavenly Father also will do to you if each of you, from his heart, does not forgive his brother his trespasses" (Matt. 18:21-35).

For closer examination, let me divide this text into four segments to help us see the potent truths revealing the importance of a disciple's spirit of forgiveness.

Nice Try, Pete! (vv. 21,22)

The setting for Jesus' lesson is a follow-up question Peter asked immediately after the Master had talked about forgiving people who violate you or have a fault that offends you (see Matt. 18:15-20). Peter, feeling generous in the wake of Jesus' call to graciousness, asks, "Then, Lord, shall I forgive *seven* times?"

Don't make the mistake of thinking that wasn't a quantum leap for the big fisherman. To Peter's understanding, seven times was more than twice anything he'd ever been taught. You see, the rabbis of the day taught that God Himself didn't forgive more than *three* times! On the basis of their interpretation of Amos' prophecy, in which God said He would judge the nations "for three transgressions . . . and for four" (Amos 1:3,6,9,11,13; 2:1,4,6), the ancient teachers concluded that if God Himself comes down heavy on the fourth violation, the teachers of the Law had no obligation to be any more patient than that. So *seven* times seemed more than generous to Peter!

But Jesus comes back with a stunning statement in which He essentially says, "Stop counting, Peter." The Lord's declaration of "seventy times seven" obviously isn't a recommendation to set up a transgression tote board and notch every grievance (to 490?) until we can justify retaliation or rejection. Instead, He's calling us to forgiveness as a way of life—He's calling us to the spirit of forgiveness.

The 100-Million Dollar Man (vv. 23-27)

Jesus' disciples are called to a lifestyle of forgiveness as a principle of discipleship. This principle is rooted in the lesson that because we have all been so *greatly* forgiven, we are logically obligated to *be* forgiving. When Jesus says, "The kingdom of heaven is like this," He is invoking this principle upon all of us who have been born again into that domain—His kingdom of love (see John 3:3).

If God said, "I forgive you," to a man who hated his brother, and if (as is impossible) that voice of forgiveness should reach the man, what would it mean to him? How would the man interpret it? Would it not mean to him, "You may go on hating. I do not mind it. You have had great provocation, and are justified in your hate"? No doubt God takes what wrong there is, and what provocation there is, into the account; but the more provocation, the more excuse that can be urged for the hate, the more reason, if possible, that the hater should be delivered from the hell of his hate, that God's child should be made the loving child that He meant him to be.

GEORGE
MACDONALD
SCOTTISH NOVELIST AND POET
1824-1905

His parable shows the amount of money owed by the first servant to be an unpayable debt. The man is a mere daily wage earner, whereas his debt—calculated by today's economic conversion rates and assuming the talents in the story were gold—is at least $100 million. The man could never hope to pay it off! This is the story equivalent of our being absolutely lost in sin apart from God's forgiveness through the cross of Jesus.

The master's initial decision to sell the man and his family into servitude and liquidate his assets (see v. 25) is not intended to be a picture of God's style in handling our indebtedness. Rather, Jesus uses the custom of his day to illustrate the binding, destructive potential of human helplessness outside God's grace.

And then the grace flows!

The total and complete wiping away of all indebtedness, the freeing of the man in response to his cry and by reason of his master's compassion—this is as dramatic a statement as we'll ever find of God's forgiveness to us through Christ.

Here is a megamillion-dollar man, many times more miraculous in his restoration than the fabled technological recovery of TV's "Six Million Dollar Man." The servant is *freed*—a masterpiece story-painting of God's infinite forgiveness. Like our freedom in Christ, His freedom is complete, undeserved and restorative.

The 99¢ Store Frame-Up (vv. 28-30)

The stark contrast which follows is meant to shock us. The man who was forgiven a fortune virtually races to claim a mere pittance from a fellow servant. He drives the man to his knees, choking him as he demands payment. The sum owed was probably about $50. At most, by any estimate, the debt couldn't be more than three months' salary. In other words, it was an amount that *could* be paid *if* . . .

But there are no ifs in the unforgiving servant's system. He not only shows himself to be small in soul but also stupid in style. He throws his fellow servant into the debtors' prison—a place where the jailed man can do nothing to change the financial facts of his circumstances. Here Jesus illustrates the way unforgiveness freezes the relational possibilities between us and those we don't forgive. When I cast into irons any present problem or stress between me and another, nothing can change. This dynamic is lived out every time I react to an attitude or deed that hurts me and I bind the person to it—that is, I decide, *If that's the way they're going to be, then that's the way it's going to be!*

The cheapness of the forgiven servant, wholly forgetting the enormity of the forgiveness that has been shown him, ends in a 99¢ Store frame-up. He jails another servant who ought to have been given the same wealth of forgiveness he had received. He might have instead seen himself as being freed to free others, but he didn't.

The Double-Disaster Ending (vv. 31-35)

Jesus concludes the story with a two-edged truth, the full implications of which are rarely understood.

First, He uses the action taken by the master of the servants
to indicate both what unforgiveness does and does not do. When
the merciful master learns what the forgiven servant has done, he
is enraged and delivers the man to be tortured until he should
pay all of the original debt. The master does *not* revert to his original judgment, that the man and his family be sold into slavery
and endless poverty. In other words, Jesus does not say that being
unforgiving reverses our salvation and returns us to a course
leading to eternal judgment. What He *does* say is powerful, as it
relates to psychological and physiological facts we know about
human beings.

As surely as "torturers" (literally, bill collectors) will regularly exact payment from the unforgiving servant from now on, so
the spirit of unforgiveness takes a sure and torturous toll on our
bodies and souls. Doctors, psychologists and psychiatrists all
have noted that the vast majority of human ills are related to
repressed attitudes of bitterness, resentment, unforgiveness,
hate, anger, self-pity and self-centeredness. All these converge in
the picture of unforgiveness Jesus draws, and the price is clearly
taught: Unforgiveness exacts its toll on our lives, bodies and relationships for as long as we carry that wearisome spirit. God says
so (see v. 35).

But there's a second seldom-noted but disturbing fact that
we must take away from this story: As the story ends, the second
servant is still in debtors' prison.

Why? Because his situation had nothing to do with his relationship with the master. His imprisonment was the result of a
dispute that was strictly between him and the unforgiving servant. While we can speculate that the unforgiving servant may

have seen his folly and repented of this action, Jesus leaves the story at this point. He does so for a reason.

You see, dear fellow disciple, you and I need to apply the lesson ourselves. Whenever we have left a relationship on the shelf—as I did with Joe—we need to let the Holy Spirit bring our folly into the light.

Where are we placing *our* fellow servants?

Do we allow them within the circle of forgiveness we have received? Or are they left outside? Do we ignorantly reserve our rights, administrating our own private counterjudgments? Do we insist on returning something of unforgiveness as payment in kind for the injustice, unkindness, rejection or disfavor we have been shown?

The principle applies deeply—right on through to attitudes we hold toward people simply because we don't like the differences in their style, manner of expression, doctrine, worship, ethnicity or culture. The fact that they are fellow servants ends up making little difference because of the capacity of an unforgiving servant to forget the grandeur of the virtually incalculable grace he or she has been shown.

But that attitude isn't unbreakable.

The lesson isn't unlearnable.

Jesus taught His disciples the need of this discipline, and He can break any bonds of unforgiveness that we invite Him to shatter. The freedom is joyous, and the *healing* power is absolutely glorious!

And so it was with Joe and me.

THE REST OF THE STORY

It was August, the summer following the Valentine's Day massacre of the spirit of my unforgiveness.

That Sunday night, Anna and I had come home from church. The kids had gone to prepare for bed, Anna to the kitchen for a snack and I to the bedroom to change into something more relaxing. And then the phone rang.

It was Joe. "Hi, guys!" he greeted us brightly, as Anna and I had both picked up the phone simultaneously. He didn't take long to get to the point.

"Jack, Anna—I just wanted to call you both tonight, because I felt you'd want to be among the first to know." He paused, then he almost shouted: "I came back to the Lord today!" He was jubilant. He was free.

I was weeping, laughing and praising God at the same time!

We visited for some time, and before concluding the call we had a holy reunion around the throne of God. But when I put the phone down, I lay back on the pillow in our bedroom. I thought, pensively and heartsearchingly, *Lord, could it be that my unrecognized attitude of judging Joe because he rejected me had somehow bound him away from a spiritual breakthrough—until I became forgiving and lovingly prayerful?*

I didn't receive an answer, until I later discovered this text in Matthew—and the servant left in the debtors' prison.

I realize that each person is responsible for his own relationship with God. And I realize that it isn't my call or mission to impose guilt on you if you have failed somehow and succumbed to unforgiveness the way I had. But you and I both are mutually responsible to take the gospel to nations and people who will never know Christ unless someone accepts the responsibility to reach them. If we do, they'll be saved. If we don't . . . ?

And if that question remains in the mission of world evangelism, perhaps it's equally true that forgiveness only flows where God can find forgiven people to dispense it. That seems to be exactly what Jesus says:

If you forgive the sins of any, they are forgiven them; if
you retain the sins of any, they are retained (John 20:23).

The message—no, the *mandate*—to become forgivers as we've
been forgiven is absolute for us as disciples of Jesus. You and I
are called to *never* withhold a largeness of attitude or forgiveness
of spirit toward anyone else. Jesus wouldn't want it.

And the Joes of this world can't live without it.

We cannot attain to the understanding of Scripture either by study or by the intellect. Your first duty is to begin by prayer. Entreat the Lord to grant you, of His great mercy, the true understanding of His Word. There is no other interpreter of the Word of God than the Author of this Word . . . in the influence of His Spirit. Believe this on the word of a man who has experience.

MARTIN LUTHER, 1483-1546

———⊷⊶———

PRINCIPLE

Persistence on a daily pathway—progressing through the Bible though beset by distraction and irregularity of schedule—is not only essential; but it also can be joyous! God's Word is the ever-available supernatural source for faith, strength, wisdom, growth and freedom in Christ. There is no substitute for its power to nurture, counsel and sustain.

———⊷⊶———

PRACTICE

I invite you, dear reader, to laugh with me at my struggles to stick with an every-day, through-the-Word-in-a-year schedule. Along with the laughter, join me in the greater joy of examining the realities undergirding our call to regular feeding and growth.

FEEDING ON THE WORD OF GOD

*Man shall not live by bread alone, but by every word
that proceeds from the mouth of God.*

MATTHEW 4:4

To begin, we all know and agree that the Word of God is absolutely essential to our personal lives and that it will only find its place there on the basis of our making a choice to read the Word daily and our exercising that duty.

No argument.

But let me invite you to take a brief, tongue-in-cheek digression—a confession of sorts. This humorously registered complaint is a look at the real human frustration I've experienced (and I dare say I have *lots* of company) in trying to keep up with those "Through the Bible in a Year" reading plans. I recently "confessed" this problem to my congregation:

> I think I've read the first 30 chapters of Genesis a hundred times! How many times have you restarted?
>
> Of course, we all need a really good Bible-reading program. Absolutely. But that three-chapters-a-day-and-five-on-Sunday plan? I doubt it was even developed by a Christian! (Remember, "tongue in cheek.")
>
> Anyone who's an active churchgoing Christian would *never* suggest you read more on a Sunday than other days. My heavens! You're already so busy with

church and everything else for God that by the time you get home Sunday night, you're glad to get *anything* read before you collapse! The whole day's been "shot to heaven"! (Stay with me, please.)

"Well, I'm going to read through the Bible this year," I said with New Year's dedication, and I *did!* That is I did manage to complete my three chapters on January 1—a monument to spiritual discipline, seeing as I was bleary-eyed from football games by the time I got ready for pre-bedtime reading. (Not to mention I was doubly exhausted due to my short-night's rest after faithful participation in my congregation's New Year's Eve midnight Communion service!)

But I stuck with it, and I chalked up three more chapters the next day. Only 363 days to go (including 52 Sundays of five per day), and I'm *home!* However, things vary from day to day—at least with me. How about you?

Day three, I woke up late. My body's starting to reel from the accumulated impact of two weeks of holiday eating up one side of the table and down the other. So I only read two chapters that day: *I'll catch up tomorrow*, I promised myself. But what really happened? Four chapters the next day? Nope, this turned out to be another two-chapter day by reason of a late wake-up, but I still feel reasonably successful—only two chapters behind, but that's OK. *I'll do five tomorrow.* Except, then I remembered: Tomorrow is Sunday! Now, it'll take seven to catch up.

Now it's Sunday night. What a great day with God and His people! Loaded with the Word and fellowship. Tired. "Well, Lord, forgive me, please. I was so busy today, could I just read three chapters? That's as many as most days, God. Okay?"

It's wild, brother! You should be feeling pretty good about life. You've read the Bible every day and read no less than two chapters any day, but here you are starting the second new week of the year and feeling semicondemned because you're already four chapters behind!

You know how it goes, don't you? C'mon! It's happened to you sometime!

By the time you arrive at January 20th, you look at your reading chart. *I'm 17 chapters behind!* Guilt territory. Even though you've read the Bible *every day,* "the plan" still has you feeling like a failure. So you decide, *Okay, this Saturday I'll catch up. I'll read the 17 chapters.* But of course, you have to make it 20, because there are three chapters for *that* day, too. You start early and give it your best. But while reading, you become fascinated with a side study—using your concordance, searching the Word, enjoying its wealth! And time runs out, so it turns out you *only* read 15 chapters.

Well, reading 15 chapters in one day should be one of the triumphs of your life, right? *But I'm still five chapters behind . . . and the next day is Sunday! Let's see, five plus five chapters equals 10, and I'll be home late from a day of worship and . . .* and so it goes.

Well, forgive my amusement at my own frustrating efforts. I don't know whether or not this reflected your experience, but I've shared this with enough people to learn it's something of a syndrome of the sincere.

Please understand that my humorous elaboration of personal frustration certainly isn't meant to discourage regular Bible reading. *Never!* But I do want to encourage the discouraged.

Truth, not eloquence, is to be sought for in Holy Scripture. Each part of the Scripture is to be read with the same Spirit wherewith it was written. We should rather search after profit in Scriptures, than subtelty of speech. Search not who spoke this or that, but mark what is spoken. Men pass away, but the truth of the Lord remaineth forever.

THOMAS À KEMPIS
1380-1471

Certainly it's a marvelous and worthy goal to read through the Bible every year, and I come close to (if not completely) fulfilling that goal most every year. But I want to lift up your heart by assuring you of this: We all have difficulty keeping a perfect pace, and I don't think guilt should ever become added baggage to the already demanding (and appropriate) goal of reading God's Word daily.

As we look at the place of the Word in the private devotional life, may I share with you a simple personal guideline that I have found works? It's worked for decades in my Christian walk, and I've recommended it to thousands. How do I keep from failing to read God's Word every day? I simply *don't turn out the light.* That's right. For me, that last action of the day has become "impossible" without my reading the Word. It's as though I'm saying, "This light doesn't go *out* until His light goes *in!*"

Of course, you may employ

other means, patterns, reminders and times. Many read the Word first thing in the morning, and I'm often there with them, too. But personally, I have found that in the morning I am too often tempted to substitute devotional reading of the Word for devotional time in prayer with the Lord. So I usually read my Bible in the evening.

Whatever your chosen milieu, the issue is that you establish the habit. The time and the coverage are yours to determine. And whatever difficulty you may have in becoming a faithful Bible reader, press forward. It's a most essential discipline to master, and we need *at least* to establish the habit of reading chapters (plural) almost every day.

THE VALUE OF A BIBLE-READING HABIT

Let's get serious for a moment and look at why we need the Word of God in our lives. You may want to jot down these key principles on the blank front or back page of your Bible as a reference point and reminder that God's Word is essential to *everything* in our lives, for *every* issue of life is covered by the truth and wisdom contained in this precious Book.

God's Word Ensures Certainty About Your Path

"Then I would not be ashamed, when I look into all Your commandments" (Ps. 119:6). The word "ashamed" as used here literally means "I won't be embarrassed." In other words, "I'm *not* going to come up short, because I have respect for Your Word in its entirety, Lord." His Word will help me to avoid confusion and embarrassing stumbling about in my life.

God's Word Gives Direction About Your Path

"Your Word is a lamp to my feet and a light to my path" (Ps. 119:105). Simply giving the Word of God a place in your life every day is taking an oath of allegiance: "Lord, Your Word is foundational and a priority in all matters of my life." This acknowledgment invites His direction:

> In all your ways acknowledge Him, and He shall direct your paths (Prov. 3:6).

Notice that direction from God's Word is both immediately at hand and revelatory of that which is distant. When the Bible says, "Your Word is a *lamp* and a *light,*" the Hebrew words are the equivalent (in today's technological terms) of saying, "You'll have a flashlight in one hand and a giant spotlight in the other." Both aspects of my pathway come into view: *details* for today and *discernment* for tomorrow.

God's Word Gives Wisdom About Your Path

"The law of the LORD is perfect, converting the soul; the testimony of the LORD is sure, making wise the simple" (Ps. 19:7). The word "simple" here makes an honest reference to an inexperienced person—it is not a condescending slur, as though the person were being stupid or ignorant. Just as the Bible points the way to wisdom (both for today's immediate situation and for the long-range path we're to pursue), here the Word is promised as a resource providing wisdom for things we face with which we have no experience. This does *not* mean that for every question we face, we will find an immediate answer. It means as I feed on the Word daily, the wisdom I need for living my life will distill in my soul. Let me elaborate.

I've learned that regular reading seldom gives me a shot of perceived wisdom each day. However, I've found that the Holy Spirit has a way of causing me to receive wisdom as a *deposit*—not so much in phrases or words but, rather, in the elements of wisdom. The nutrients of God's truth are made to flow into my spirit. Then when I need them, though I may not remember chapters and verses, the strength and the wisdom needed will be available by reason of the spiritual resources inside me that have accumulated through faithfulness to this spiritual habit.

Some time ago a friend of my mother said to her, "Dolores, I feel so stupid when I study the Word of God. I just don't seem to remember anything at all."

Quite wisely, my mother responded, "Lou, do you remember what you ate for breakfast on Tuesday, three weeks ago?"

Her friend looked at her, rather stunned, and replied, "Well, no, I don't."

Mama explained, "It still supported and nourished you, didn't it?"

Get the point? Just keep reading the Bible. You may not remember everything, but *the Word is flowing into your spirit*. And as it does, it's giving you abiding strength and sustenance as you simply obey and read.

Jesus said, "Man shall not live by bread alone, but by every word that proceeds from the mouth of God" (Matt. 4:4). *There* is your daily bread! We can expect strength today, not only because of today's reading; but there's also a component of strength available because of what we "ate" on Tuesday, three weeks ago, when we fed on the Word of God!

God's Word Ensures Our Victory in Our Pathway

There's something about our giving place to the Word of God that ensures not only today's nourishment but also our *success*!

> This Book of the Law shall not depart from your mouth,
> but you shall meditate in it day and night, that you may
> observe to do according to all that is written in it. For
> then you will make your way prosperous, and then you
> will have good success (Josh. 1:8).

Joshua had just taken over the reins of leadership from Moses, following the great deliverer's death. Can you imagine the impossible (from Joshua's perspective) challenge he faced? But God gave Joshua a promise of His presence and His purpose, linking them to His precepts.

The promise of success, through God's promised presence and unfolding purpose being realized in our lives, is offered to us today on the same terms. Keep the Word in your mind, in your heart and on your lips! The Word *works*—richly and mightily:

> Let the word of Christ dwell in you richly (Col. 3:16).

> So the word of the Lord grew mightily and prevailed (Acts 19:20).

God's Word Keeps Us Pure in Our Path

Another benefit of reading the Bible is the power of the Word to keep us pure.

> How can a young man cleanse his way? By taking heed
> according to Your word. . . . Your word I have hidden in
> my heart, that I might not sin against You (Ps. 119:9,11).

The Word is not just a spotlight that shines outward and gives direction; it's also a searchlight that shines inward, prompting, correcting, adjusting and instructing me. Jesus prayed, "Sanctify them by Your truth. *Your word is truth"* (John 17:17, emphasis added). Earlier He declared, "You shall know the truth, and the truth shall make you free" (John 8:32). God's Word not only purifies us *from* sin; it is also a preventative measure *against* sin!

When Jesus faced temptation in the wilderness, as Satan came not only to taunt but also to destroy Him, Jesus responded to every thrust of the adversary's lies with a counterthrust of the sword of the Spirit—the truth of the Word of God.

D. L. Moody said of the Bible, "This Book will keep you from sin, or sin will keep you from this Book." The Bible is not only a resource book that provides us certainty, direction, wisdom and victory. It is also a "resistance book" that helps keep us pure.

God's Word Keeps Us Alert to the Times

"And everyone who has this hope in Him purifies himself just as He is pure" (1 John 3:3). The Scriptures sometimes speak to us with flashing warning signs that show us the nature of our times and signal us to stay ready for Jesus Christ's return. With our eyes on the Lord—loving His appearing (see 2 Tim. 4:8)—the Word is key to keeping us from falling asleep in the darkening hour, as the spirit of our age attempts to lull us into carnal torpor and sensual indulgence. The Word will keep us walking a pure path and maintaining an alert stance, strong and ready to do battle in the name of the Lord.

The promise of Jesus' imminent return is real! And steadfast, daily, heartwarming, self-examining, faith-building, soul-purifying reading will keep us ready.

> But take heed to yourselves, lest your hearts be weighed
> down with carousing, drunkenness, and cares of this life,

and that Day come on you unexpectedly. For it will come as a snare on all those who dwell on the face of the whole earth. Watch therefore, and pray always that you may be counted worthy to escape all these things that will come to pass, and to stand before the Son of Man (Luke 21:34-36).

God's Word Is Our Shield of Faith

"So then faith comes by hearing, and hearing by the word of God" (Rom. 10:17). Faith is our fundamental means of resisting the devil—the shield we use to withstand him. Faith defends against attack as an implement that is forged and fashioned by our hearing and reading the Word of God.

But remember, fellow learner: "Hearing" is not a passive, sit-in-church-on Sunday-and-you're-done proposition. Rather, to hear the Word means to (1) *feed* on it as a steadfast practice and (2) *heed* it as a sensitive hearer and doer of the Word (see Jas. 1:22).

Earlier, we discussed this kind of hearing (that is, hearing the voice of God) as a practice foundational to all disciplines. But the starting place for life-growing faith is in the *heeding to reading*—obeying His *leading unto feeding* as one of Jesus' sheep. That will bring fullness of faith and build us into victors, from sheep to soldiers!

Feed and heed! That's our call to this resource above all resources, the standard by which everything is gauged, the foundational footing for everywhere you may walk in life—the living, eternal, holy Word of God.

Live *in* it.

Live *by* it.

Live *through* it.

Daily.

Never . . . think we have a due knowledge of ourselves until we have been
exposed to various kinds of temptations, and tried on every side. Integrity on
one side of our character is no voucher for integrity on another. We cannot tell
how we should act if brought under temptations different from those we have
hitherto experienced. This thought should keep us humble. We are sinners, but
we do not know how great. He alone knows who died for our sins.

JOHN HENRY NEWMAN
ROMAN CATHOLIC CARDINAL, 1801-1890

PRINCIPLE

Contrary to Western intellectual thought, God is not known by way of the mind but by way of the heart. Through our intelligence we may deduce things about Him, and our minds may study reality as revealed by Him. But God can only be truly known in person and in intimacy by those who seek Him with all their hearts. Once He is met and known, our advancement on the path to spiritual maturity and personal effectiveness is realized in the fullest way only as we maintain in humility and childlikeness a discipline of purity, a totality of heart-yieldedness and a vulnerability to the Holy Spirit.

PRACTICE

Starting at the Bible's first reference to integrity of heart, we will examine the richness of the concept and finally, close with a lesson I learned early from my mother's words, "In front of Jesus."

MAINTAINING INTEGRITY OF HEART

Blessed are the pure in heart, for they shall see God.

MATTHEW 5:8

Every year at my birthday I receive hundreds of cards, not only because I serve a large congregation but also because of a tradition that has accidentally evolved. About 20 years ago, on the Sunday following my birthday, I read aloud at the morning service from a couple of humorous greeting cards I'd received. The congregation so enjoyed this reading that I did the same thing the following year. And so, without aforethought or intention, a tradition was born.

And so it is today that a host of people in our congregation watch the racks all year looking for the funniest card they can find, hoping their card might selected to be read aloud. Each birthday is loaded with laughter for me and, on the Sunday following, for the congregation.

One card I recently received read as follows:

I hear you're telling your *real* age.
What honesty,
What humility,
What integrity.

(turning to the inside)
What a memory!

There was a virtual explosion of laughter when I read that one.

From that light mention of integrity as a point of beginning, let's turn to a weightier discussion of the subject. I would like to deal with integrity of heart and the maintenance of such as a basic discipline of Christian living.

The Bible tells us that from out of our hearts all issues of life are distilled and resolved (see Prov. 4:23). This truth is key to a promise of great significance and hope for every disciple. In essence it says that if I can learn to be absolutely, totally, completely and unreservedly *honest to God*—up front with every dealing of His Spirit in my heart, responding to His promptings and submitting to His corrections—there is immeasurable joy to be found and immeasurable sorrow I'll be spared. Furthermore, immeasurable blessings will be poured out on others through the channel of a heart that remains unpolluted and available to the Holy Spirit's pure grace-workings!

So this study deals with the matter of our openness and transparency before God, and we start by looking at this idea of integrity.

An Introduction to Integrity

The notion of integrity of heart in the Word first appears in the telling of an incident in Abraham's life:

> And Abraham journeyed from there to the South, and dwelt between Kadesh and Shur, and sojourned in Gerar. Now Abraham said of Sarah his wife, "She is my sister." And Abimelech king of Gerar sent and took Sarah.

But God came to Abimelech in a dream by night, and said to him, "Indeed you are a dead man because of the woman whom you have taken, for she is a man's wife."

But Abimelech had not come near her; and he said, "Lord, will You slay a righteous nation also? Did he not say to me, 'She is my sister'? And she, even she herself said, 'He is my brother.' In the integrity of my heart and innocence of my hands I have done this."

And God said to him in a dream, "Yes, I know that you did this in the integrity of your heart. For I also withheld you from sinning against Me; therefore I did not let you touch her" (Gen. 20:1-6).

The background to this episode centers on an agreement made years before between Sarah and Abraham. Because of her beauty, he had asked Sarah that if in their nomadic travels they were ever to come to a place where his life might be jeopardized because a regional king might kill Abraham in order to take Sarah for his harem, they would claim *not* to be husband and wife. It certainly sounds peculiar today, but their agreement, while less than faith-filled, was somewhat understandable given the context of that ancient culture.

In any case such a confrontation *had* happened, and Abraham had said, "She is my sister." So Abimelech, king of Gerar, is about to take Sarah for himself.

But God steps in!

In this gracious action of divine intervention to protect Sarah and Abraham from their foolishness and lack of faith, the Lord comes to Abimelech in a midnight visitation. Notice how quickly God gets his attention.

"You're a dead man."

Immediately, Abimelech protests the charge, appealing to his innocence of intent to take another man's wife, and he appeals to God with these words: "I did this in the integrity of my heart."

Look at that exchange again.

God says, "You're a dead man because . . ." In response, Abimelech replies, "But I was acting in *integrity*." In other words, "I didn't get into this situation by means of a calculated plan for evil."

This brings us to the point where God says—listen closely now—"I know. That's why I'm here to correct you."

It's important for us to recognize this text as more than a story. We're being introduced to the principle of integrity of heart, a truth being dramatized for us in a way that establishes the concept in the Word of God.

There's a simple principle of Bible study usually called *the law of first usage*. It's impressively consistent, in that it simply notes that the first time you encounter an idea or principle in the Bible, you will generally find its first usage defines the idea's usage throughout God's Word—the concept will be consistent in intent and meaning throughout the Scriptures, as it is found in its first occurrence.

This passage in Genesis 20 is the first time the word "integrity" actually occurs in the Bible, and the incident is freighted with insight. It begins with an illustration of how all of us are vulnerable to confusion and mistakes, to being misled or to becoming the victim of someone else's manipulations. Like Abimelech, without our awareness and completely outside our intent or cooperation, we may become trapped.

But here the Bible discloses a life principle: God is prepared to guard and deliver an honest heart—a heart of integrity—and to defend that heart against the possibility of delusion. This powerful truth holds the promise for each of us that the Lord will keep our life "on-line" amid the swirling seas of confusion seemingly omnipresent in our world. Through the simple but demanding discipline of our constant walk in integrity of heart, God reveals He will protect and defend us from devices of evil or detours of self-confusion.

Integrity of heart can be further understood as we look at other uses of this concept in the Scriptures. Let's look at Psalm 25:21:

Let integrity and uprightness preserve me, for I wait for You.

At the time David wrote this, the boundaries of his kingdom had broadened to such a degree that he had no way to adequately defend its entire perimeter. Here he shows that he's made a choice, as though saying, "Lord, there aren't enough troops to guard every border, so I'm asking: Let my integrity of heart before You become my defense." The implication of this request would create an agreement something like this:

Lord, I'm going to walk before You in absolute obedience—to do what I perceive to be Your will and to respond to Your dealings with my heart. And then in exchange, Lord, I ask You to so lead me, in the context of my honesty of heart before You, that I will be guided by Your providence and wisdom and protection so that I will remain wise in administrating my borders—that I shall be kept by *Your* counsels as my defense against my enemies.

The Lord did that during David's lifetime—at every point. As long as David walked in integrity of heart, he was preserved. When he violated it, he not only stumbled but also his kingdom boundaries were penetrated.

For contrast—and a severe lesson—look at Solomon, David's son.

In 1 Kings 8:12-53, we are told how Solomon prayed at the time the Temple was dedicated. He humbly opened himself to the Lord in a beautiful way, revealing the same spirit and attitude of his father, David. He asked for God to perpetuate his kingdom, much the same as He had for David. In response to his prayer, the Lord establishes His terms:

> Now if you walk before Me as your father David walked, in *integrity of heart* . . . then I will establish the throne of your kingdom over Israel forever (1 Kings 9:4,5, emphasis added).

Through these biblical examples we see integrity as a key to three blessings: prevention, preservation, perpetuation. For example:

- Abimelech was *prevented* from becoming "entangled" because he walked in integrity of heart.
- David's boundaries were *preserved* as long as he retained integrity of heart.
- Solomon was promised *perpetuation* of his kingdom if he maintained integrity of heart.

God *will preserve* us—you and me! He *will prevent* us from evil involvements that could cause us to stumble. He *will perpetuate* the good blessings He intends for us. But the clear condition for all this is that we maintain integrity of heart.

WHOLE OF UNDERSTANDING

In the English language, "integrity" is a word related to a number of other familiar ones, terms which help us see the fuller dimension of its implications. "Integrity" is built from the root idea in our English word "integer." As most of us learned in elementary math, an integer is a whole number, such as 1, 2, 3 or 4—that is, whole numbers as opposed to fractions. That's "whole," as in the idea of completeness or entirety of a thing or a number.

Similarly, we find the idea of wholeness in such words as "integration" (fitting together ideas or units, as opposed to fragmentation) or in "disintegration" (the fragmenting of what was once complete or together). Both "integer" (a whole number) and "integration" (parts being made into a whole) illustrate the concept inherent in "integrity."

This word describes uncompromised character, an unjaded soul, an unsullied heart and an undivided mind. It requires the maintenance of one's heart in entirety before the Lord. As David said, "Unite my heart to fear Your name" (Ps. 86:11). In other words, *God, draw the strands of my heart so firmly and in such reverence before Your throne that I will be kept wholly and entirely aligned with You.*

Wholeness or integrity of heart is also expressed in Psalm 119:10:

With my whole heart I have sought You;
Oh, let me not wander from Your commandments!

Here again the psalmist is crying out, "Lord, don't let me come apart at the seams through parceling out segments of my heart or through letting portions become sliced off when I'm tempted to allow myself to yield to circumstances that conspire to divide my attitude. I want my heart, my *all*, to be kept *whole* and thereby *holy* before You, O Lord!" Can you hear the spirit of this word, loved one? Wholeness of the heart. Entirety!

This is precisely the concept implied in the Hebrew word *tom* and in the Greek New Testament counterpart *eirene,* the word for "peace." Colossians 3:15 says, "And let the peace of God rule in your hearts." The words apply the same spirit as found in the summons of Ephesians 4:30: "And do not grieve the Holy Spirit of God, by whom you were sealed for the day of redemption." These texts show how the Holy Spirit will signal us anytime we grieve Him by starting to fragment, or segment, parts of our heart rather than keeping it all entirely under God's rule.

Similarly, the mind or our thoughts can be divided through doubt or self-justifying rationalizations when we're tempted to compromise, or sin. But being honest to God when He deals with your heart observes a fundamental discipline that will *prevent* us from confusion, *preserve* us against the enemy's encroachment and *perpetuate* us in God's blessing.

DIPLOMACY OR DEPENDENCE?

Evidence of what happens when integrity is gradually eroded is found in what happened to Solomon. Remember, the Lord had promised him, "Solomon, if you will walk in integrity of heart as your father David did, I will perpetuate your kingdom." Did He? Would God keep His promise—a promise contingent upon the maintenance of integrity of heart? Let's look at what happened.

Before his son's rule, during David's reign as king, he had said, "Lord, I don't have enough troops to guard all our borders. I will walk in integrity of heart and trust You to be my defender." Unfortunately, Solomon chose a different approach. Solomon began negotiating treaties with neighboring nations in order to protect his borders. Rather than depending on the Lord and walking in humility before Him, Solomon attempted to build his own defense by means of political gamesmanship, relying on his own skill at manipulating people. He began negotiating treaties, and every time he struck a treaty with a nearby nation—trying to cover his borders—he married a princess from that nation. With the arrival of each new princess, a new pagan god was welcomed to Jerusalem and enshrined in honor of the treaty. In time these shrines filled Jerusalem, compromising the integrity of the worship of the one true God and bringing decay to the kingdom.

The same thing can happen to you or me today.

Once you and I begin trying to manipulate our situations, once we begin trying to negotiate with human wisdom or reasoning rather than depending on the Lord as our defender and guide, inevitably our hearts will be splintered in fragments because integrity of heart has been sacrificed on the altar of human expediency. How can we guard against such loss?

I am bold in saying this, but I believe that no one is ever changed, either by doctrine, by hearing the Word, or by the preaching or teaching of another, unless the affections are moved by these things. No one ever seeks salvation, no one ever cries for wisdom, no one ever wrestles with God, no one ever kneels in prayer or flees from sin, with a heart that remains unaffected. In a word, there is never any great achievement by the things of religion without a heart deeply affected by those things.

JONATHAN
EDWARDS
1703-1758

One day as I was studying this word "integrity" (*tom*) in the Hebrew text, not long after this concept struck my heart as a mandate for the disciple's walk with God, I was astounded by a discovery while looking up the occurrences of the word in a Hebrew concordance. There I learned that the plural of the word "tom" is *Thummim*. Interestingly, this word is retained in its Hebrew form in most English translations.

For example, in describing the breastplate of the high priest, the Old Testament tells us:

> And you shall put in the breastplate of judgment the Urim and the Thummim, and they shall be over Aaron's heart when he goes in before the LORD. So Aaron shall bear the judgment of the children of Israel over his heart before the LORD continually (Exod. 28:30).

Notice, the Urim and Thummim were to be over Aaron's heart whenever he went before the Lord. How striking a picture! What can it depict?

To this day, no one knows what the "Urim and the Thummim" actually were. Rabbinical literature doesn't specify. But what we do know is that "Urim" means "lights" and "Thummim" means "completenesses, perfections or wholenesses." In their commentary on Exodus, Keil and Delitzsch give us an idea as to what was being commanded in this passage:

> What the *Urim* and *Thummim* really were cannot be determined with certainty, either from the names themselves or from any other circumstances connected with them. . . . This expresses with tolerable accuracy . . . illumination and completion. . . . Now if we refer to Numbers 27:21, where Joshua as the commander of

the nation is instructed to go to the high priest Eleazar, that the latter may inquire before Jehovah, through the right of Urim, how the whole congregation should walk and act, we can draw no other conclusion, than that the Urim and Thummim are to be regarded as a certain medium, given by the Lord to His people, through which, whenever the congregation required divine illumination to guide its actions, that illumination was guaranteed. . . . Consequently the Urim and Thummim did not represent the illumination and right of Israel, but were . . . a pledge that the Lord would maintain the rights of His people, and give them through the high priest the illumination requisite for their protection. Aaron was to bear the children of Israel upon his heart, in the precious stones to be worn upon his breast with the names of the twelve tribes. The heart, according to the biblical view, is the centre of the spiritual life, not merely of the willing, desiring, thinking life, but of the emotional life, as the seat of the feelings and affections (see *Delitzsch bibl. Psychologie,* p. 203). Hence to bear upon the heart does not merely mean to bear in mind, but denotes "personal intertwining with the life of another."[1]

The Urim and Thummim were consulted whenever the high priest needed to go before the Lord and ask, "What is Israel to do in this situation?" How were the Urim and Thummim consulted? It is said that the priest would go into the holy place and stand outside the curtain of the Holy of Holies, which could be entered only once a year. And there the high priest would humbly inquire of the Lord God of Israel, "What should we do, Lord? What is Your will for us?"

See it, please. The high priest had gone past the brazen altar in the outer court, past the laver into the holy place, past the table of showbread, past the lampstand, and had worshiped at the altar of incense. Now, standing in worship before the Holy of Holies, by the Urim and the Thummim, an answer was given.

What was it—light? Did a holy glow appear on the chest of the priest? What was the completeness, the Thummim?

While we don't know precisely, the Lord gave complete and wholehearted assurance—apparently by the radiant warmth of His presence and a sense of peace—as to what action was acceptable and what wasn't. If this kind of guidance was available to priests under the Old Covenant, what can this mean for us today?

Our understanding is enriched when we remember that under the New Covenant, God has made every one of us "priests" (Rev. 1:6). As such, we have been assigned prayer and worship ministries; but none of our responsibilities exceeds the stewardship we've been given in monitoring our own hearts before God. That's why Colossians 3:15 commands, "Let the peace of God rule in your hearts." Let His peace—the warm inner glow born of an uncompromised, unsegmented wholeness—be the arbiter or umpire of our decisions, our situations and our life's issues.

We aren't to negotiate by, or with, the flesh.

We aren't to try to work things out by our own wisdom.

We aren't to contrive or compromise.

The Holy Spirit will signal our hearts at needed times with a very quiet inner sense, either of confirmation or correction. When He is correcting, you may sense in your soul a kind of "ping," and you'll know the Lord is "checking you." I learned that phrase as a boy: "If the Lord checks you . . ." I came to understand it to mean somewhat the same thing as when a person "checks" another in a chess match, blocking forward progress.

So the Lord will block us when we are moving in a direction He knows is wrong or unwise for us.

We may not know why the Holy Spirit deals with us as He does at times, and often we'll be tempted to push ahead anyway. But a wise, responsive heart of integrity will sensitively welcome His correction. For example:

- You're engaged in conversation when you suddenly realize that you have turned a conversational corner that is about to compromise your honesty or purity. Let Him stop you when your heart signals that "ping" of correction.

- You're making plans and you sense the inner stoplight of the Holy Spirit turning red. Immediately cease that direction in your planning and trust that the Lord has a better plan for you.

- Perhaps you've finished the plans. You *had* sensed a check in your spirit but felt embarrassed to turn back and say, "This really is not a wise move. I need to stop what I was going to do and go in a different direction." It's still not too late. Be willing to be honest with yourself and others. If you fail to respond to God's checking, or blocking, of the situation, it will eventually cause frustration for everyone involved. So learn to respond quickly. In every situation pray, *Lord, I want to be corrected and taught by You.*

I WAS ABOUT 11 YEARS OLD

The importance of integrity of heart was impressed upon me as a child. I first related the following incident in my book *A Man's Integrity*, a study of how men can develop godly character.

When I was a boy, my mother had a special means for dealing with each of us children—my brother, my sister and me. Whenever Mama thought any of us might be tempted to be less than truthful because of the pressure of a situation where possible correction might have followed an honest confession, she would take a precautionary step. Instead of simply asking, "Did you do (such and such)?" she would preface the question with a statement. This statement had a very sobering effect on me, because it so vividly taught the reality of my accountability to be truthful in the eyes of God. Mama would say, "I'm going to ask you a difficult question, Jack. But before I do, I want to say, I'm asking it in front of Jesus."

She wasn't playing games.

She wasn't threatening.

She wasn't using a religious ploy to cajole us.

In our house we took the Lord seriously. Our home was a happy place to live, but we really believed in the genuine nature of God's love, His kindness, His blessing, His salvation in Christ and the beautiful truth of His Word. And when Mama would say, "in front of Jesus," a powerful image would come to my mind.

We all knew that God is everywhere, all the time. But there was a unique sense of the immediacy of the living Lord when those words were spoken. I could imagine Jesus seated on a throne immediately to my left as I stood face-to-face with my mother and prepared to hear the question she had to ask.

A Visit to Richie's House

I had come home from a friend's house one afternoon, having spent most of the morning with Richie—a kid a few months older than I who lived across the street. We played together a lot, so there was no reason for Mama to think anything unusual had happened when I (then 11) came home that day.

But the next morning, as I was about to leave for school, I learned that my mother had *felt* something upon my return home from Richie's the day before.

I had just finished my breakfast and was about to leave the kitchen to get my school things when my mother turned from the kitchen sink, and while drying her hands, said, "Jack, I want you to wait a minute. I need to talk with you." Her voice had that tone all children recognize in their parents when the issue is sobering and the consequences might be undesirable. I stood there, nervously waiting for what she was going to say.

"Son, when you came home from Richie's yesterday, I had a very strange feeling go through me." She paused thoughtfully. "At first I didn't know what to do about it. Then I prayed last night, and I believe the Lord showed me simply to do what I'm doing right now. Jack, I want to ask you what happened at Richie's house yesterday. And I'm asking this *in front of Jesus*."

I froze where I stood. It was one of those crystalline moments that seemed as though it could be shattered by a whisper. On the one hand I knew what happened at Richie's house, and I knew I didn't want anyone else to know. And on the other hand—there to my left—the throne of my living Savior, Jesus Christ, was as real to me as though I were standing in heaven itself.

I began slowly . . . awkwardly . . . guiltily.

"Well, Mama," I said rather quietly and with some hesitation. "When I was at Richie's, after we'd been playing in the living room for a long time, he said to me, 'C'mon into my room a minute.' When he said that, he kinda laughed and looked around to see if his mom or dad were anywhere they could hear. Right then I felt something bad was about to happen, but I went with him anyway.

"When we got to his room, Richie closed the door. And then he opened one of the drawers in the chest there. He reached way in the back and brought out a tiny little telescope."

I hesitated again, feeling the embarrassment of the confession I was about to make.

"But Mama, it wasn't a telescope." I paused again. Waiting. Not wanting to go on. "Instead, Mama, when you looked into it, there was . . . a naked woman." My eyes were moist. I looked into the face of my mother, feeling ashamed.

"What did you do, Son?" she inquired.

"We laughed," I admitted.

"How did you feel then?"

"Mama," I said with sincerity, "I felt bad."

"Then, Son, what do you want to do now?"

I walked toward my mother, whose arms opened to me as I did, and I said, "I want to pray, Mama."

And we did.

And although that event took place more than five decades ago, at its root is a truth that has always continued to be just as alive and present today as it was then: *I am living my life in front of Jesus.*

I'll never know how many things that morning's confrontation and confession may have saved me from as a teenager and young man. Just as surely, I don't really know how much of anything I have done may have contributed to some degree of fruitfulness in my life and ministry.

I do know this: I know that there are no limits to what God can do *in* a life, what He can do *through* a life and what He can grow *around* and *within* a life when it's lived in front of Jesus.

That's the place where integrity of heart will always be sustained. For our consciousness will be trained on Him, not on people or things. And with Jesus in view, all fruitfulness and fulfillment are certain to be realized with time, however tempting or trying the path.

Let's live out our lives that way. In front of Jesus.

WHAT IS "BEING SPIRITUAL?"

Among the funniest things I've ever seen is someone trying to "be spiritual."

You've probably seen it, too.

I'm not talking about hypocrisy—the phony front that seeks to cover insincerity. No, I'm referring to the labored efforts of some sincere people who mean to serve Jesus with all their hearts, but feel obligated to communicate some special aura of "godliness."

The attempt shows up in several ways: an affected tone of voice; a glazed look to the eyes; a certain posture of the head that appears to be trying to balance a halo; a . . . well, just an altogether unnatural bearing that tends to become at least humorous, and at worst, spooky.

Nevertheless, there is a recovery in progress today . . . a recovery of true spirituality. It is being experienced in people who are learning that true sanctification is letting the Holy Spirit make you the true you. That doesn't mean you don't need to be transformed—regenerated—born again. You do! Jesus said so in John 3:3,5. Second Corinthians 5:17 makes it clear that the true you is a new you.

But that "new" is neither "gooey godly" or "pious prude." When the touch of Jesus comes on a person, He sets in motion the redemption program—that is, His "bringing back from what wasn't" into the "realizing of what was supposed to be."

That's His plan in "redeeming" . . . to take each individual trait in each person's created uniqueness and recover anything that's been lost—erased by sin or failure. God's purpose for each of His beloved sons and daughters is regained. Redemption buys back God's best, after human failure has worked its worst.

This isn't something you strive to accomplish, but it is something you have to want—to open up to—to permit the glory of God's grace to achieve in you.

The elements of "being spiritual" have been listed for ages in every kind of disciplinary guide ever formulated or published for believers. These include prayer, Bible reading, fellowship with believers, self-denial, growth in the things of the Holy Spirit, self-less giving and serving others.

True spirituality, however, somehow just happens. Like fruit on a tree. Like flowers on a plant. Like grapes on a vine . . . that's it. Grapes on a vine.

> Abide in Me, and I in you. As the branch cannot bear fruit of itself, unless it abides in the vine, neither can you, unless you abide in Me. I am the vine, you are the branches. He who abides in Me, and I in him, bears much fruit; for without Me you can do nothing (John 15:4,5).

Jesus says, "If you abide in Me, it will all begin to happen." Association—a constant link—with Him will produce dissocia-tion—a consuming break—with everything in us that isn't of Him. And when He makes us what God the Father designed us to be, we are relieved of the task of trying to appear as something we thought we ought to be.

I've never seen a grape with a hernia . . . or with a halo, for that matter. They neither grunt nor glow . . . they just grow.

That's what "being spiritual" is all about.[2]

True spiritual power of the Christian order is a kind of possessedness. It arises
in and flows through a life hid with Christ in God. Its source is the grace of
our Lord Jesus Christ, and the potency of the Holy Spirit.

SAMUEL M. SHOEMAKER
1893-1963

PRINCIPLE

Nothing in the believer's life is more essential to his or her becoming a daily, fully empowered replication and representative of Jesus Christ than being and keeping filled with the Holy Spirit. From Pentecost until our Lord's return, the Church's commission is to be "endued with power from on high" (Luke 24:49), "do business till I [Jesus] come" (Luke 19:13), "go into all the world"(Mark 16:15) and to experience "the Lord working with them and confirming the word through the accompanying signs" (Mark 16:20). Fulfillment of this rather full mandate is only possible through being baptized in the Holy Spirit and continually being freshly filled with His love and power.

PRACTICE

I invite you to answer here with me a summons that came to my own soul—one that is fully consistent with all our Savior said and all the Early Church experienced. It is a call to abandon ourselves to the Holy Spirit—to yield to His fullness, to open to the worship He enables, to utilize the full prayer resources He supplies and to exalt and minister the works of our Lord, Jesus Christ.

ABIDING IN THE FULLNESS OF THE SPIRIT

*He who believes in Me, as the Scripture has said, out of his heart
will flow rivers of living water.*

JOHN 7:38

I had just taken a seat on the platform, having introduced the
guest speaker who would be addressing our congregation that
day. Before the guest said even one word, the Lord had preached a
sermon to me. The phrase whispered into my soul puzzled me,
but it also profoundly impressed me: *Open to the spirit of enthusiasm.*

I knew this was a prompting from the Lord, and I didn't
argue with Him. But I was surprised He would say *that* to me.
Why? Because I think of enthusiasm as being superficial exuberance—people merely "whooping it up" into a kind of frenzy akin
to standing on the bleachers and screaming. Now, I'm capable of
that, too, because I am quite a sports enthusiast. But I also knew
something much deeper about the word "enthusiasm," and it
was that knowledge which sobered my response and stirred my
expectancy.

"Enthusiasm" is derived from the Greek word *entheos*, meaning "God is in them." The idea of enthusiasm, historically and
etymologically, has to do with a person being so full of God (or,
in the pagan world, the gods or the muses) that behavior is dominated by *Him* in a holy sense (or by *them* in a pagan or even
demonic sense). In short, enthusiasm makes a person dynami-

cally or vibrantly alive with a resource from a realm other than the natural.

As I thought through the word the Lord had whispered to my soul—*Open to the spirit of enthusiasm*—I knew He was seeking to address something of my inclination toward reservedness. I sensed that He did not want me to become so sedate, in a "cool" response to Holy Spirit fullness, that I overlooked the place, purpose and desirability of the vibrant and the vital—the *expressive*, if you will. He wasn't issuing a call to superficial exuberance, but neither was He preempting the expressively exuberant.

Are you tempted to keep your cool, to maintain control even while asking to be made "full of God"? I'm inclined to believe the temptation to maintain respectability is more dangerous than we might think. We are surrounded by sophistication in our culture; and in our religious traditions and observances it becomes too easy to somehow suppose that God equates our reserve with reverence, as though we were trying to impress Him—or worse, others—with our style.

But God isn't impressed by either intellectual or emotional sophistry. And as for society, it's a question of degree: How far will you go to please the world? We may feel we must pamper worldly-mindedness by cooling our praise in church. But inevitably, the flesh will prompt us to cool our message, our convictions and our lifestyle as Christians. So before you dampen your praise or demonstrative worship or witnessing, consider just how much "cool" you think will ultimately satisfy the world.

Of course, neither is God impressed by the raucous. A call to enthusiasm isn't a call to stylized fanaticism. There is no special merit in being rowdy or noisy for its own sake. If neither the fanatical nor the opposite (the sophisticate's mannered, near-snobbishness of religious reticence) is impressive to God, what might I need to open myself to?

My sense of God's answer to that question pointed to my need to learn a readiness to make myself fully open to the spirit of enthusiasm—in readily allowing, indeed welcoming, the overflow, the vibrancy, the warmth and expressiveness of Holy Spirit fullness to find release in and through me.

As a result of that evening's platform encounter, I was drawn to John 7:37-39:

> On the last day, that great day of the feast, Jesus stood and cried out, saying, "If anyone thirsts, let him come to Me and drink. He who believes in Me, as the Scripture has said, out of his heart will flow rivers of living water." But this He spoke concerning the Spirit, whom those believing in Him would receive; for the Holy Spirit was not yet given, because Jesus was not yet glorified.

John explains the context in which the incident occurred, and he tells us Jesus was referring to something that would happen a considerable time later.

This event—the celebration of the Feast of Tabernacles—took place about six months before the crucifixion of Jesus. In ancient Israel this annual feast commemorated the Israelites' journey through the wilderness after their release from bondage in Egypt. Can you imagine the hubbub in the marketplace in Jerusalem? Tents and little shelters built from branches (which gave the feast its name) were erected in the streets to house the families that had come from all over Palestine to celebrate and worship. The shelters served more than a ceremonial purpose; during this early autumn season they would need them for nighttime rest as well.

Among other traditions, the feast included the great water-pouring ceremony, which reminded Israel of God's supernatural provision of water in the desert wastelands. Rabbinical writings tell us that the priests used huge urns from which they poured water from the top of the Temple steps. It was a very dramatic moment when the water splashed and cascaded down the steps as the Jewish people lifted up high praise to God and rejoiced.

The last day of the feast climaxed a week of celebration. So it was, on the last day, that Jesus rose to shout, "He who believes in Me, as the Scripture has said, out of his heart will flow rivers of living water." His proclamation was a call to Holy Spirit fullness. Jesus said "rivers of living water" are to flow from His followers. Please notice His use of the plural "rivers."

John explains that Jesus was making a prophetic forecast about the *future* and the Spirit's work within us. Jesus was describing a way of life for us *today*. He pointed beyond an initial experience in the Holy Spirit—beyond being baptized in the Spirit—to a lifestyle bathed in Spirit fullness to the point of day-to-day overflowing.

All these thoughts converged as I read that passage, drawn by the Lord's word: *Open to the spirit of enthusiasm.* When this occurred I certainly wasn't stagnant in my walk with the Lord. I had determined years ago to seek to abide in the fullness of the Spirit, and I was reasonably current in the sense of His blessing and presence. But it seemed as though the Lord was showing me something, that the intensity of today's times required my expanding in His fullness all the more: I was to let the Spirit-fullness already in me increase and abound!

As a result of this encounter and my sense of the Holy Spirit's desire to pour out a special refreshing on me—on us!—I began to think, *What might these "rivers" be which the Lord wants to release in us?* I took time to examine that thought in God's Word and came up with these "rivers," streams of refreshment and mightiness the Holy Spirit waits to unleash within any of us who will allow Him to do so.

Rivers of Worship and Praise

On the Day of Pentecost, the followers of Christ "were all filled with the Holy Spirit and began to speak with other tongues, as the Spirit gave them utterance" (Acts 2:4). Peter explained this Spirit-begotten language after their praises to God brought acknowledgment from onlookers that the disciples were speaking of "the wonderful works of God" (Acts 2:11).

Notice the relationship of a spirit of praise and worship to the exercise of speaking with tongues. It's often debated as to whether speaking with tongues is or isn't a sign of being filled with the Holy Spirit. This is not the subject of the book you are now reading, but I do believe the Word of God makes it clear that this language of praise is a dynamic *privilege* available to people who are filled with the Spirit.

Rivers of Witness

Fresh entheos fullness will bring a vibrant readiness in the believing disciple to joyously tell others about Jesus.

> But when the Helper comes, whom I shall send to you from the Father, the Spirit of truth who proceeds from the Father, He will testify of Me. And you also will bear witness, because you have been with Me from the beginning (John 15:26,27).

> He will glorify Me, for He will take of what is Mine and declare it to you (John 16:14).

Rivers of Ministry

There are ministry gifts waiting to flow from the Spirit-filled believer to people who are in torment or pain and in need of divine grace. Jesus Himself said:

> And these signs will follow those who believe: In My name they will cast out demons; they will speak with new tongues. . . . They will lay hands on the sick, and they will recover (Mark 16:17,18).

Rivers of Gifts (by the Spirit)

The Holy Spirit wants to give through us more and more of the Father's goodness and blessings. Freshness and renewal in the Spirit will rekindle our availability to His gifts, that we might function as His delivery personnel according to His will, becoming avenues through whom rivers of gifts may flow to others. First Corinthians 12:7-11 speaks of the Holy Spirit within, manifesting His presence by the distribution of gifts according to His will.

Rivers of Intercession and Prayer

The Holy Spirit wants to advance us in power and warfare prayer. We will certainly encounter many situations about which we may not know *how* to pray, but His fresh flowing will assist us.

> Likewise the Spirit also helps in our weaknesses. For we do not know what we should pray for as we ought, but the Spirit Himself makes intercession for us with groanings which cannot be uttered. Now He who searches the hearts knows what the mind of the Spirit is, because He

makes intercession for the saints according to the will of
God (Rom. 8:26,27).

Rivers of Fruitfulness

There will never be any divine legislation against the fruit of the
Spirit, and there will never be any human law against the beauty
of God's grace in people. Rivers have always increased fruit bearing in the agricultural realm, so we are wise to open new flood-
gates of the Holy Spirit's flowing in our lives to see abundant
fruit in our character and conduct.

> But the fruit of the Spirit is love, joy, peace, longsuffer-
> ing, kindness, goodness, faithfulness, gentleness, self-
> control. Against such there is no law (Gal. 5:22,23).

Rivers of Peace and Strength

The Bible points to the distinct flow of Holy Spirit-enabled
prayer as a means of edification: "He who speaks in a tongue edifies himself, but he who prophesies edifies the church" (1 Cor.
14:4). No apology is needed, for this isn't a self-serving exercise;
it's necessary.

God's Word says we are being edified as we worship supernaturally before God's throne in our times of private devotion, and
such sensitive employment of this resource deserves to be com-
mended. As God knows, we need all the edification we can get.

Rivers of Revelation

The apostle Paul said, "I'm praying for this—that God will give you
the Spirit of wisdom and revelation" (see Eph. 1:16,17). Why?

Good, then, is this water, even the grace of the Spirit. Who will give this Fount to my breast? Let it spring up in me, let that which gives eternal life flow upon me. Let that Fount overflow upon us, and not flow away.

St. Ambrose
339-397

Because refreshing and renewal from the Holy Spirit *always* bring fresh vision and insight as to God's purpose in our lives:

> The eyes of your understanding being enlightened; that you may know what is the hope of His calling, what are the riches of the glory of His inheritance in the saints (Eph. 1:18).

OPEN TO THE SPIRIT OF ENTHUSIASM!

Here is a scriptural reminder of our need: "Be filled with the Holy Spirit" (Eph. 5:18). It's God's intent. Spirit-fullness in the New Testament is emphasized as a recurring necessity. For example, see both Peter and Paul. Each were Spirit-filled but were filled afresh for special situations (cf. Acts 2:4 with 4:8; Acts 9:17 with 13:9).

The same is true with the Early Church community, which was filled initially (see Acts 2:4,38) and refilled later (see Acts 4:31). So *keeping on* in the Spirit's fullness—opening to the Spirit's entheos rivers—is very scriptural.

In order for us to gain a sense of the ways in which the Spirit fills us, join me in a study of several verbs used in the book of Acts—words that describe our being filled to overflowing by the Holy Spirit. He didn't choose these different words simply to provide a variety of expressions. Rather, they reveal to us the full range of experiences in the Holy Spirit.

We Are Baptized in the Holy Spirit.

In ancient times the Greek word *bapto* was used in a number of interesting ways. It essentially described something that was immersed. Examples include a sunken ship, a drowned person, the dipping of a morsel of bread in a drink and the dyeing of a garment.

Jesus said, "For John truly baptized with water, but you shall be baptized with the Holy Spirit not many days from now" (Acts 1:5). In using the word "bapto" to describe our entry into the dynamic of His fullness of life and power, Jesus chose it to describe living in the fullness of the Spirit. Today the Lord might say, "I want to flood all compartments!"

Furthermore, He was calling for a change, just as a dyed garment takes on an entirely new dimension of beauty that wouldn't be present otherwise. Being baptized in the Holy Spirit brings new qualities to our life and character. So when we talk about baptism in the Spirit, these kinds of immersions show us what we were intended to experience.

The Holy Spirit Comes Upon You.

Jesus said to His disciples, "You shall receive power when the Holy Spirit has come upon you; and you shall be witnesses to

Me . . . to the end of the earth" (Acts 1:8). The chief idea in *eper-chomai* ("come upon") relates to a whole new set of circumstances coming upon us. In other words, the Holy Spirit wants to reshape our *perspective* (on the world), our *passion* (for the lost) and our *pointedness* (in focusing on human need). The Spirit's power also clothes *(enduo)* us in power (see Luke 24:49, *NIV*)—another kind of "coming upon" us of His resources of enablement.

The Holy Spirit Is Poured Out.

In Acts 2:17, Peter quotes from Joel's prophecy about the coming of the Holy Spirit: "And it shall come to pass in the last days, says God, that I will pour out of My Spirit on all flesh."

What happens when the abundance of water behind the dam courses through the generator within the dam and releases energy? A roaring sound? Perhaps. But the purpose of this engineering marvel is not to generate the thunderous sound as the water rushes through the sluice gates but, rather, to generate *power* and *light* to serve cities miles away. By the releasing of the potential within the dam, energy is channeled for the intended purpose.

God would say to us, "Live in the fullness of the Spirit of enthusiasm and let the rivers surge in and through you to light the world wherever you go, day by day."

We Are Filled.

"And they were all filled with the Holy Spirit" (Acts 2:4). In the Greek language, the verb *pleroo* ("to fill") was not used except to indicate an overflow. The word means there's more than enough! As a "rivers of enthusiasm" reminder, our Lord is saying, "Don't ever depend upon the scanty resources of experiences past, because My *abundant* resource is always available. There always will be *more than enough* of My Spirit working in you, but you need to remain open to His renewing, refilling workings!"

Paul's call to be "praying always with all prayer and supplication in the Spirit" (Eph. 6:18) by continuously being "filled with the Spirit" (Eph. 5:18) provides us with direction to ensure our keeping this overflow occurring. Our wise response—praising with "psalms and hymns and spiritual songs, singing and making melody in your heart to the Lord" (Eph. 5:19)—gives place to this pleroo overflowing fullness of the Spirit. Let every day be filled with more than enough. For example, drive to work singing, praising the Lord en route as you let the language of praise overflow.

The Holy Spirit Falls Upon Us.

"While Peter was still speaking these words, the Holy Spirit fell upon all those who heard the word" (Acts 10:44). *Epipipto* (Greek, "to fall upon") suggests one of the loveliest ideas I've found concerning being filled with the Spirit. Do you remember Jesus' story of the prodigal son? When the boy returned, the father met his son with great affection—he "fell on his neck," embracing him with joyous acceptance (Luke 15:20).

This "falling upon" is not a ludicrous scene of a man falling out of a tree on a passing boy. It is the picture of a man coming and capturing his long-lost son in a grace-filled embrace of gratitude and affection. And that's the same word that is used in Acts 8:16: "For as yet He had *fallen upon* none of them. They had only been baptized in the name of the Lord Jesus" (emphasis added). Here we find believers who had been baptized in water as an action of obedience following their repentance and faith in Christ, but they had not yet received the fullness of the Spirit. Some follow-up work was needed. This underscores the need for what is often called a "second work" of grace—not because our salvation is enlarged or expanded upon but, rather, because our enablement for power-filled service is a distinct action in God's order of grace-works.

The same is true today. The Holy Spirit wants to fall upon us and capture us in the embrace of heaven, to catch us up in the fullness of God's love, so that His great love may overflow to others as we touch them in His name.

We Receive Him.

"Then they laid hands on them, and they received the Holy Spirit" (Acts 8:17). Interestingly, *lambano* (Greek, "receive") conveys both the ideas of giving *and* receiving. In short, everything ultimately relates to our willingness to be open to Him, to allow His power, grace and glory to flow all ways—to and from us!

Dear one, I'm presuming you're like me, wanting this openness to be manifest in your life and attitude. I've addressed you as one who does not need to be convinced of the value of the fullness of the Holy Spirit—as a brother or sister who desires *everything* Christ Jesus promises His disciples.

Do you agree with me that if our Lord might say, "Open to the spirit of enthusiasm," He has a reason? Well, I knew He said it to me, and since the Bible enjoins us to keep on being filled with the Holy Spirit, I think we can all assume it's a lifelong discipline for every earnest believer.

To observe it, let me invite you to join your heart with mine in receiving the constant reminder that we all need continuous refreshings and refillings with the Holy Spirit. At the very least, the Church's first Pentecost deserves an annual revisitation; yet surprisingly few congregations even note the day, much less celebrate it. In contrast, however, for more than 30 years we have led the flock of The Church On The Way in an annual post-Easter pattern of seven weeks of study, prayer and praise-filled pursuit of personal renewal in the Holy Spirit's fullness. The objective: to keep full of the Spirit that we may demonstrate His love and power to that world each one of us touches.

Each Pentecost Sunday (usually late May or early June), we climax our annual four-day *Conference on Spirit-Filled Living* with a grand opportunity for all who know Christ to be (1) baptized in water, if they have not; (2) baptized in the Holy Spirit, if they have not; and (3) be dynamically refilled with the Holy Spirit, for we *all* need that! The spirit of this passion is summarized in the following article I wrote for our congregation for a Pentecost Sunday. It's an exhortation recounting a dream I had and the hunger it renewed in me.

LORD, BAPTIZE ME AFRESH

It's a fitting day for each of us to review the subject of *baptism*—both in water and in the Holy Spirit. On this day of celebrating Pentecost—the day the Church was born—I want to invite you to stand with me and listen again to the holy thunder in Peter's words:

> Repent, and let every one of you be baptized in the name of Jesus Christ for the remission of sins; and you shall receive the gift of the Holy Spirit. For the promise is to you and to your children, and to all who are afar off, as many as the Lord our God will call (Acts 2:38,39).

Two "calls" grip my heart today; the first call is to me, but let me extend the second call first. It's to you—to each of you with whom I share the life of Jesus. I'm calling *you*, in His name, to be baptized afresh! This, of course, does not mean we attempt a reenactment, but that we open to a revisitation—open to a renewal of all the dynamics that are inherent in the Father's purposes in these two baptisms.

Obviously, this call is pointedly directed to you if you have yet to obey our Lord Jesus' commands to both be *baptized in water* (see Matt. 28:19; Mark 16:16) and *baptized in the Holy Spirit* (see John 7:38,39; 20:22).

Then, with that call to you who have been, and to all who need to be, baptized according to the Scriptures, I am answering a call myself.

It was a dream. Hundreds of people were being baptized in water, and I was rejoicing with the throng present. Then a whisper came to my heart: *You go and be baptized, too.* I immediately recognized this was not a condemning directive, as though my baptism in water years ago had somehow become invalidated. But in sensing a call to obedience, I immediately responded, went to the dressing room and then to the baptistry.

In my dream, I found I was the last person to step down toward the waters, but mysteriously, there was no water in the baptistry. I looked at the pastoral staff members who were baptizing, and one of them said, "The last person took the last drop—there's no more water left."

Such dreams are often confusing, but the message of this point was clear to my soul: I was being called to be refreshed in the truth that we are all called to live in the stream of the Spirit, a river that never runs dry. And if we ever step out of the stream, *there isn't any resource on Earth we can step into to substitute for the Holy Spirit's river of life and power!*

It was a dramatic reminder: I was called to be renewed in all the meaning of my water baptism *now* and to be refilled with all the dynamic of my experience in the Holy

Spirit—*this* Pentecost Day! So join me—for Jesus' sake and under His lordship.

Let's be baptized afresh![1]

Such a heartfelt passion must be sustained in our lives as disciples of Jesus. Otherwise, "Christian living" becomes reduced to simply being nice girls and boys for Jesus, rather than living in the timelessly available resources of the Holy Spirit,

fully empowered as *witnesses* of His life, love and power;

fully representative as *evidence* of His character, conduct and grace;

fully endowed as *agents* of the kingdom of God, manifesting its presence because we are living in its King's fullness and

fully released as *worshipers* and *intercessors* who both praise and pray with the spirit and with the understanding (see 1 Cor. 14:15).

It can never be said too often: This discipline is essential to fulfilling all the others. Keep on being filled with the Holy Spirit. Amen!

ABIDING IN THE FULLNESS OF THE SPIRIT

O Holy Spirit come upon me,
Pour Your grace and Your glory all around,
Now as at Jesus' feet I'm bowing,
Let the fire of heaven flood this holy ground.
As I lift my hands in full surrender,
Fill my life and lips with highest praise:
Come fill me now! Come fill me now!
Holy Spirit come upon me,
That my Jesus—my Lord and Savior, Jesus—
Fill all my ways, all my days.

J.W.H.

The man must be patiently cultivated to produce a wise man; and the wise man must be tested and tried if he is to become righteous, and the righteous man must have substituted the will of God for his individual will, if he is to become a godly man.

HENRI FRÉDÉRIC AMIEL, 1821-1881

———∞∞∞———

PRINCIPLE

As disciples of Jesus we have been called to the One who, being in the form of God, did not consider it something to be held onto to be equal with God, but taking the form of a servant, "humbled Himself and became obedient to the point of death, even the death of the cross" (Phil. 2:8). The pathway of biblical surrender is not only to yield to Christ as Lord but also to follow Him as the Servant who "came not to be ministered unto, but to minister, and to give his life a ransom for many" (Matt. 20:28, *KJV*).

———∞∞∞———

PRACTICE

Few ideas concerning discipleship in Christ have been more distorted than the concept of submission. We are never called to a reduced existence; instead, we are called to a liberating refusal of a carnal insistence on "my own rights."

LIVING A LIFE OF SUBMISSION

Then Jesus said to His disciples, "If anyone desires to come after Me, let him deny himself, and take up his cross, and follow Me."

MATTHEW 16:24

Several years ago, one of America's best-known industrialists began attending our church. He had visited for several months before we met. As we conversed one day, he was very candid when he told me about laughing at himself and his early encounters and responses while attending our services.

He had received Christ elsewhere, and he was young in the Lord when he first arrived. God used our ushers as instruments to touch this man's life—and deeply! I serve a church that has been blessed with remarkable growth, so our ushers have been given specific instructions for greeting people upon their arrival in the sanctuary: Contrary to people's tendency to sit in the back row, our ushers are expected to lead—not herd, but "persuasively invite"—people to the yet unfilled row closest to the front of the sanctuary. This allows latecomers to be seated without distracting other worshipers, and people generally respond very positively to the request.

So it was that when the business leader spoke with me one day, he said he had always cooperated out of courtesy. Then he added, "Pastor, you have no idea how it rankled me. I detested being told by those people where I should sit. Everything in my life until then had always been under *my* control. Having the direction of a sizable industry, I am accustomed to having it exactly the way I *think* it should be, *when* it should be and *how* it should be."

He laughed at himself and continued, "But I didn't realize this wasn't the way the Lord wanted my life. He used some very ordinary men, some dear brethren, who earlier in my life I would have virtually scorned as people I could buy and sell a thousand times over. Now the Lord used them to remind me of how much I need to learn the spirit of submission."

He not only accepted sitting where ushers told him to sit while pretending a good attitude, but he also learned what it meant to have a *genuine* spirit of loving, trusting submission to Jesus Christ. He saw the situation for what it was: a call to yield to Him.

Frankly, there aren't many of us as readily willing to acknowledge our need of this discipline. In the judgment of some, "a life of submission" sounds like a page out of a handbook for membership in a religious order—a call to a monastery. In fact, in much of today's Church, many have almost sanctified the notion of autonomy, of independence, of "I can do just about whatever I want because of my freedom in Christ." Such self-justifying claims, asserting a supposed right to bypass learning the practice of submission, take different forms: "God is no respecter of persons." "I am as important in God as anyone." "Submission breeds mind-control cults."

On the face of it, you can't deny the element of truth these words represent; but the *spirit* of submission is the issue, not parroted words about "freedom."

In terms of spiritual reality, we *are* made free. But liberty in Christ isn't a program of perpetuating self-rule in the soul. Our freedom is meant to (1) free us from practicing sin, (2) free us from smallness of soul and (3) free us from a Lone Ranger kind of independence that proposes "me" as the single-handed controller of everything in life. The spirit of submission, lived out on biblical terms, proposes that God could, in fact, use other people to teach me, to surround me with supporting insights to help me grow. The spirit of submission brings me to a voluntary willingness to be accountable to others, even if that means I'm exposing myself to the possibility that at times these others will correct me in the spirit of love. These valuable, life-building assets can only be realized if I am willing to learn the spirit of submission. But "submission" is a scary word for so many of us.

THE MEANING OF SUBMISSION

"Submission" is often thought to imply a situation in which one person might be exploited, manipulated or dominated by another. But let's clear the air with an understanding of its true definition.

First, please read with me:

Now when Jesus had entered Capernaum, a centurion came to Him, pleading with Him, saying, "Lord, my servant is lying at home paralyzed, dreadfully tormented."

And Jesus said to him, "I will come and heal him."

The centurion answered and said, "Lord, I am not worthy that You should come under my roof. But only speak a word, and my servant will be healed. For I also am a man under authority, having soldiers under me. And I say to this one, 'Go,' and he goes; and to another, 'Come,' and he comes; and to my servant, 'Do this,' and he does it."

When Jesus heard it, He marveled, and said to those who followed, "Assuredly, I say to you, I have not found such great faith, not even in Israel!"

Then Jesus said to the centurion, "Go your way; and as you have believed, so let it be done for you." And his servant was healed that same hour (Matt. 8:5-10,13).

Here is a starting point for understanding the true idea of submission, because the *heart* of the concept is there in the centurion's response to Jesus and the actual *way* in which the word was originally derived is present in the setting itself.

The centurion is a military man, a leader of men who says, in essence, "Jesus, I say to my soldiers, 'Do this and they do it.' I am a man *under* authority and I *administer* that authority according to a specific order of *alignment*." He understands that *his* submission—alignment with the authority placed over him— is the source of the power available to him. The centurion's power and authority are not self-derived, but rather, they are

We are all pencils in the hand of a writing God, who is sending love letters to the world.

MOTHER TERESA
1910-1999

delegated through an appointed order (military or governmental in this case). His acceptance of his role as a "submitted" man has given rise to the power and authority he exercises.

The centurion recognizes in Jesus another man of great authority and power, and he uses his position to make an analogy. His observation is essentially this: "Jesus, just as I have military *authority,* I know You have authority in another realm. So all You need to do is to speak a word." Now listen to Jesus' perspective: "I have not found such great faith, not even in Israel!" Jesus not only confirms the man's faith, but also commends the man's perspective, understanding and spirit.

That same hour, the centurion's servant is healed. Jesus exercises power over affliction and brings healing to the servant. Seeing this, the thoughtful soul must inquire:

- What possibilities are waiting to be released in me if I, too, learn God's order of alignment for my life and I voluntarily submit to that order?
- Just as the centurion submitted to an order of authority over him, what are those points of divinely appointed order I need to accept?
- Just as the centurion's servant was healed by a release of faith (born of one man's perspective on true humility) and Christ's power (born of true authority), who or what in my life awaits healing, wholeness or recovery—if true submission is learned?

Let me assure you, a glorious release of power awaits the individual, the congregation—indeed, the whole Body of Christ—if and when we learn to submit ourselves to one another in the fear of God (see Eph. 5:21)—i.e., in reverence for His divine order.

The meaning of the word *hupotasso* (Greek, "to submit") is unquestionably related to military structures. It was used to refer to an arrangement of troops under proper order—each private, corporal, sergeant, lieutenant and captain relating correctly right up the line through majors, colonels and generals to a commander in chief. In such military regimentation the structure is not designed to reduce the significance of any person or to inflate the importance of another. Rather, the structure is designed to *assist* the effectiveness of all, to *assure* the interests of all and to *assemble* the whole of the body to resist and overthrow the enemy.

The Bible is very clear: There *is* a God-ordained order for every facet of our lives. None of us is simply a stand-alone believer. Of course, we do stand individually responsible before God in terms of our relationship and accountability to Him. But the life of the believer is constituted of many other dimensions, relationships and factors. And even in the realm of our spiritual relationships—to a church, to fellow Christians, to ministries—it is very easy to subtly arrogate to oneself a broad individualism on the supposition that "I'm a free creature under God, and I'll do just what I want or see as best." We can be ever so nice, keeping the laws of society and even obeying the boss at work. But get us in church? The unspoken sentiment all too often is "Hey, we're all in charge here!"

But that leading industrialist I mentioned was willing to learn submission to spiritual authority—to the point of submitting to a lowly usher. He refused to retain the almost self-righteous proposition that given his lofty position in the business world, he had the right to refuse to submit in this situation. There are, in fact, certain realms of authority and accountability where our souls won't be damned if we refuse submission. But such refusal certainly can *shrink* our souls. "Unsubmission" of heart is unlike Jesus:

Let this mind be in you which was also in Christ Jesus, who, being in the form of God, did not consider it robbery to be equal with God, but made Himself of no reputation, taking the form of a servant, and coming in the likeness of men. And being found in appearance as a man, He humbled Himself and became obedient to the point of death, even the death of the cross. Therefore God also has highly exalted Him and given Him the name which is above every name, that at the name of Jesus every knee should bow, of those in heaven, and of those on earth, and of those under the earth, and that every tongue should confess that Jesus Christ is Lord, to the glory of God the Father (Phil. 2:5-11).

His example calls you and me to discover the power release and growth that will only happen in and through us if we properly learn the spirit of submission. The path down (submitting) is the way up (receiving authority). Even then, all authority in the spiritual realm is only to be exercised in the Spirit and with the attitude of a servant:

But Jesus called them to Himself and said, "You know that the rulers of the Gentiles lord it over them, and those who are great exercise authority over them. Yet it shall not be so among you; but whoever desires to become great among you, let him be your servant. And whoever desires to be first among you, let him be your slave—just as the Son of Man did not come to be served, but to serve, and to give His life a ransom for many" (Matt. 20:25-28).

Submission to God's arrangement and order is not designed to rank people above others but rather to serve the interests of all, so the whole army comes to victory. The submitted disciple learns there is a tactical advantage—a mutual protection that takes place through (1) *committed involvement* with a church family, (2) *submitted service* as a member of the Body and *(3) acceptance* of a personal *accountability* to others in Christ.

In this response to God's order, everybody wins. It is not a matter of saying, "Who's on top? Who's boss?" It's a matter of saying, "Lord, teach me my place. I humbly yield to learning, to growing. Lord, I'll even sit where the usher says!"

While society interprets "submission" to mean either subjugation or domination, it doesn't mean that at all. Subjugation and domination are what happens when one person or kingdom rules over another: One party is intimidated, plundered, mastered and then broken.

But submission has nothing to do with that, for there really isn't any such thing as *forced* submission. True submission can never be forced because, foremost, submission is an inner attitude—a heart issue. It can never be required; it can only be volunteered, given as a willing gift. Only I can choose whether or not I will submit.

Under Christ, we must learn the spirit of submission as it relates to others—others we serve with, others we serve under, others we don't want to serve at all. But willingness, humility and servanthood must be kept in view. I may *say* I'll submit; but if my heart rankles and internally resents or resists, I am not accepting or participating in the spirit of submission. And not only will I fail to garner the power God intends me to know through becoming a submitted person, I will also miss the blessing. The blessings awaiting the submitted disciple are beautifully set forth in this marvelous hymn:

Trust and Obey
When we walk with the Lord in the light of His Word,
What a glory He sheds on our way!

While we do His good will He abides with us still,
And with all who will trust and obey.

Refrain:
Trust and obey, for there's no other way,
To be happy in Jesus, but to trust and obey.

Not a shadow can rise, not a cloud in the skies,
But His smile quickly drives it away;
Not a doubt nor a fear, not a sigh nor a tear,
Can abide while we trust and obey.

Not a burden we bear, not a sorrow we share,
But our toil He doth richly repay;
Not a grief nor a loss, not a frown nor a cross,
But is blest if we trust and obey.

But we never can prove the delights of His love
Until all on the altar we lay;
For the favor He shows and the joy He bestows
Are for them who will trust and obey.

Then in fellowship sweet we will sit at His feet,
Or we'll walk by His side in the way;
What He says we will do, where He sends we will go,
Never fear, only trust and obey.[1]

We see here that true submission is more than learning the principle of submission in the texts of Scripture; it is learned in passing the tests of life. How we choose to submit in the most basic situations of our lives is the real evidence of the degree to which we have become submitted.

- As a husband, how do I relate to my wife—as a servant or as a tyrant? As a responsible leader or as a heel-dragging child?

- As a wife, how do you relate to your husband—as a supporting partner manifesting the unique sweetness and love potential in true femininity or as a complaining, controlling nag?

- As a parent, how do I relate to my children—as a role model, serving their need for a picture of what they can become? As an interested dad or mom, caring, correcting, affirming and disciplining when necessary?

- As an employee, how do I relate to my job, my fellow workers and my supervisor—as a trustworthy bearer of my share of the task? As a dependable, on-time, "you can count on me" partner or as a passive, disinterested, "only as much as I've gotta do" pain to have around? (Or, worse, as the company "religious freak" who talks a faith that does not manifest itself in daily diligence as an employee!)

- As a Christian, how do I relate to my church—as a supporting giver, an active servant, a right-spirited member, a team player with the leadership? Or do I carry such attitudes as: "I'll give, but only to what I'm interested in"? "I'll attend, but don't ask me to do anything"? "I'll be around, but I want to keep my distance"? "I'll join, but I'm reserving my right to murmur or criticize when I want"?

· As a disciple, do I accept the practical wisdom of finding a small circle of peers in Christ to whom I make myself accountable? Am I willing to stand with these people, to be mutually corrected, to be assisted toward growth in grace and to be bonded through a common, powerful love of God for strength? Am I willing to turn to these people when I need support to face trial, temptation or stressful circumstances?

A Christian man is most free lord of all, and subject to none; a Christian man is the most dutiful servant of all, and subject to everyone.

MARTIN LUTHER
1483-1546

Only by our willingness to learn and grow in these ways will we ever become all that we truly can be in Christ. Our Savior was the model of the submitted life, and yet He functioned with more dynamic authority and dominion than anyone in all history. Look at Him.

He stooped to a manger on Earth, though rightfully the King of the universe.

He was baptized to serve the Father's purpose, though onlookers might have assumed it to be an act of repentance.

He accepted rejection without retaliating in kind.

He willingly accepted the slapping of His face and did not spit back.

He prayed, "Father . . . not My will, but Yours, be done" (Luke 22:42).

He accepted the slashing and spearing of His body and in effect said, "Father, forgive them; they don't understand" (see Luke 23:34).

Jesus submitted to people in darkness, tirelessly giving Himself to help them come to understanding. When His disciples said, "Let us call down fire from heaven on those who wouldn't let You come into town," Jesus in effect said, "No, that's not our style—you don't know what spirit you are of" (see Luke 9:54-56). He taught that the spirit of His kingdom is not to exercise power to prove you're superior or right. Rather, we are called to learn the spirit of submission, to let a grander power manifest through us—the power of love which, given time, will beget trust and responsiveness.

There are husbands who never win the spirit of submission from their wives, because they never lay down their own lives; instead, they lay down their own *laws,* demanding their own authority or supposed privileges.

There are wives who never draw from their husbands the best responses, because they are unwilling to surrender to a possibility—the possibility that, were they to show the sweet spirit of volunteered submission, they might evoke something beautiful from their husbands. But they are unwilling to risk losing control in order to secure the potential of that beauty.

As the Lord grew me (I'm afraid I was a slow learner), I gradually came to see the structure of His order and respond to it.

There is so much to be gained through a disciple's learning the biblical spirit and practical pathway of submission. And there are so many lessons and points of application that point us to that pathway.

The following outline is a resource I've used—in my work with men and also in seminars with couples and spiritual leaders—to examine the truth and path of submission.

THE CONCEPT OF SUBMISSION

I.   **The Semantics of Submission (see Matt. 8:5-10)**

A. When Jesus declared, "I have not found such great faith," He was remarking on the comment of the Roman centurion who acknowledged his recognition of Jesus' authority over sickness because of his own understanding of the principle of being set "under authority." This is the essence of the New Testament word "hupotasso," which is essentially a military word denoting order, place or rank. Translated most frequently as "submit" or "subject," the word occurs in 14 books of the New Testament a total of 44 times.

B. English terms which answer to this idea include "yielded" and "obedient." The oft-used expression "surrender to God's will" incorporates the idea of submission as an introductory act, while "walking in the will of God" conveys the idea of submission as a life pattern.

C. The term "covering" is heard much today. It is also related to the idea of order and, therefore, to submission. (Example: Ezekiel 28:14 uses the term to denote Satan's rank before his transgression.) Covering implies protection by virtue of one's yielding to, or acceptance of, an overseeing and loving authority. Therefore, in the vernacular of faith, we say we are "covered with the blood of Jesus," which affirms that we have submitted ourselves in faith to the protection that blood provides from judgment on our sins.

II. **The Significance of Submission (see Heb. 2)**

A. All sin is the resultant outflow of the rejection of one's place in God's order of things. First, Lucifer's "I will ascend," and second, Adam's seeking of knowledge not intended for him (see Isa. 14:14; Gen. 3:5,6).

B. All redemption is the resultant outflow of the submission of the Son of God to the Father's will:

1. To incarnation (see Heb. 5:5-7)

2. To identification with man (see Matt. 3:13-17)

3. To suffering in life (see Matt. 26:52-54; Heb. 5:8; 12:3)

4. To death (see Phil. 2:8; Heb. 2:9)

C. The highest of human destiny in the redemptive program of God through His Son Jesus is the *restoring of man to his intended place of authority as ruler.* Hebrews 2 develops this majestically and shows man removed from being "subject to bondage" (v. 15) and experiencing all things "in subjection" under him. Verses 9,10 clearly display that Jesus' pathway of submission—the unquestioning life of trustful obedience—leads to this rulership.

III. **The Specifics of Submission (see 1 Pet. 5)**

There are seven basic areas of life that require submissiveness on the part of mankind. Each merits a whole range of development and bears far more Scripture support than the brief list of references given here. But this simple outline serves as a framework for further study. New Testament life, in which the fullness of God's love for man has been revealed, summons submission at these levels of relationship:

A. Submission to *God the Father* (see Heb. 12:5-9; Jas. 4:6,7)

B. Submission to *the Truth* (see Rom. 10:3 on receiving God's provision of righteousness through Christ alone, without works)

C. Submission to the *Body of Christ.* This refers to:

1. Jesus as the Head (see Eph. 1:20-23; Col. 2:18,19)

2. Local eldership (see 1 Cor. 16:16; Heb. 13:17) and church government

3. Individuals of the membership (see Eph. 5:21; 1 Pet. 5:5)

D. Submission to *parents* (see Luke 2:51; Col. 3:20; Eph. 6:1-3)

E. Submission to *civil authority* (see Rom. 13:1-7; 1 Pet. 2:13-23)

F. Submission to *employers* (see Eph. 6:5-7; Col. 3:22)

G. Submission to roles as *husband and wife* (see Eph. 5:22-33; Col. 3:18,19)

IV. **The Spirit of Submission (see Ps. 37)**

Any truth can be stretched over the rack of cold, literalistic application and made into a dried hide of demanding duty. However, New Testament life is not designed to *wrap* man in newly developed legal demands but rather to *fill* man with new possibilities for living in the love of God by the outflow of the Holy Spirit (see Rom. 5:5). The enunciating of the basic-to-life principle of submission can be responded to in fear, in doubt, in presumption, in love, in trust or in understanding. To select the wise response and avoid the foolish requires a wholehearted openness toward the Holy Spirit. Only He can lead us into the living of any truth. We need to be mindful that:

A. *The Spirit of submission is not cowardly* (see 2 Tim. 1:7). He will not produce passive, insensitive saints who flop before anything in supposed submission. We are *not* to submit to:

    1. Satan (see 1 Pet. 5:8,9). For example, sin and sickness are resisted.

    2. Flesh (see 1 Cor. 9:24-27). We are to make no provision for it.

    3. Legalism (see Gal. 2:4,5). It is *always* in opposition to the gospel.

B. *The Spirit of submission is not confused* (see Acts 4:15-21; 5:26-42). This deals with the question "How does one submit to conflicting authorities?" The apostles satisfied both God and rulers, submitting unto both. They did not submit to demands of silence, but they did submit to scourging with joy.

C. *The Spirit of submission is not contentious* (see 1 Cor. 11:16).

D. *The Spirit of submission is not comparatively competitive.* Second Corinthians 1:12 warns against the ugliest aspects of a spirit of competition, while Proverbs 27:17 recommends the best aspects of "sharpening" one another by interactive activity.

Conclusion

Every earnest New Testament believer wants to be effective in ministry. Jesus has clearly encouraged our expectation of full-ministry flow in John 14:12. But the flow of *His* kind and quality of ministry requires the preparation of His kind and quality of submissiveness. Before He became the Great Shepherd, He submitted to being the Lamb of God. The course for the fulfillment of our ministries is charted by submission to that same tender walk before the Father.

We Christians must simplify our lives or lose untold treasures on earth and in eternity. Modern civilization is so complex as to make the devotional life all but impossible. It wears us out by multiplying distractions and beats us down destroying our solitude, where otherwise we might drink and renew our strength before going out to face the world again. "The thoughtful soul to solitude retires," said the poet of other and quieter times; but where is the solitude to which we can retire today? "Commune with your own heart upon your bed and be still," is a wise and healing counsel; but how can it be followed in this day of the newspaper, the telephone, the radio and television? These modern playthings, like pet tiger cubs, have grown so large and dangerous that they threaten to devour us all.

A. W. TOZER, 1897-1963

━━━∞━━━

PRINCIPLE

Here we will consider the wisdom and benefits of regularly experiencing both the private, personal presence of God and personal time and space away from life's daily demands. Without this occasional solitude, life and service will become a blare, producing discouragement, distraction and defeat. But if we will regularly implement this practice, life will be recharged with energy and spiritual dynamism.

━━━∞━━━

PRACTICE

The practice of solitude is neither an attempt to escape reality nor a retreat from responsibility. Rather, it is the biblical response to the timeless reality that the demands of duty, the swirl of activities, the pressures of circumstance and the tyranny of the urgent tend to converge on us all. In the midst of a busy ministry, Jesus established a pattern that teaches His disciples a principle that secures balance and helps us retain our priorities.

PRACTICING SOLITUDE

*Now in the morning, having risen a long while before daylight, He went
out and departed to a solitary place; and there He prayed.*

MARK 1:35

The hallmark of people who walk faithfully with the Lord for
long seasons of time—people who can experience trials beyond
anything they had known before and come through with faithfulness, stability and strength of character—is that they have
learned a simple way. In the final analysis, what truly allows these
people to live steadfastly in the things of the Spirit over the long
haul is not their ability to stand splendidly in glory moments;
rather, it's their ability to find a way through difficulties by God's
grace, having found resources of grace in ways less obvious.

Such people know the value of quietness. I'm speaking of
solitude, of waiting on the Lord as a necessary resource for dealing with the tough times in life—at *any* time. I suppose all of us
at such times wish we could "get away from it all." Of course, we
do need times to literally get away for times of recreation, and
there's no fault in that. A game of tennis, a round of golf or a
vacation in Switzerland—they're all great. But recreation, vacation or relaxation are not what I mean by solitude, although they
may at times provide a setting for it.

Still, we need to distinguish between the value of these *active*
recreational times and the value realized in the more *pensive*
order of re-creating that solitude affords. By solitude I mean
being alone with the Lord in a quiet quest for God.

We see this illustrated in Jesus' ministry. The practice of solitude was His idea, and it speaks volumes to us today:

Then the apostles gathered to Jesus and told Him all things, both what they had done and what they had taught. And He said to them, "Come aside by yourselves to a deserted place and rest a while." For there were many coming and going, and they did not even have time to eat. So they departed to a deserted place in the boat by themselves (Mark 6:30-32).

No elaboration is needed. The text is fully self-explanatory. There simply are times that we need to *stop*. Jesus noted that and called His disciples to observe a "time-out" with Him.

I was interested to discover what appears to be a companion event to this, a similar "breakaway" in Paul's life—one that could go unnoticed unless we trace the geography referenced in Acts 20:13.

Then we went ahead to the ship and sailed to Assos, there intending to take Paul on board; for so he had given orders, intending himself to go on foot.

Luke is making a simple geographic reference that in sailing from Troas, their next stop was to be Assos. But Paul goes another way. Apparently, he has said, "You guys go ahead on board. I'm going to hike to Assos, and I'll meet you there." The distance he walked was possibly 25 miles, while the ship would have sailed west, then south, then east again and around a point. The longer route for the ship's journey would take some time, so Paul apparently chose to walk. But why?

It's logical to conclude that he wanted time to be alone. He probably wasn't completely without companionship, because that would have been dangerous in those times. But you can imagine that extended journeys on ancient sailing ships meant cramped quarters in the ship's hold and even a feeling of confinement on the deck of the small craft of the day. But here was a chance to amble freely through God's creation, to breathe the refreshing air of the countryside. No doubt Paul made the journey on foot because he felt the need for a break—a change of pace.

Other examples from the Word are readily apparent:

- God's dealing with Moses became profoundly impacting and history shaping after Moses' 40 days atop Mount Sinai.
- Fleeing Jezebel, Elijah escaped into the wilderness, where he met God and rediscovered what his life was really about.
- David's flight from Saul produced some of his greatest psalms, written in a wilderness hideaway at En Gedi.
- John was exiled to Patmos where, though seemingly "out of commission," he met Jesus again and wrote the book of Revelation.

There are any number of cases—biblical and extrabiblical—where people have gone into times of solitude and, rather than *escaping* reality, they found *entrance* into it. They came freshly into the reality of God's presence and found there a renewal of His purpose for their lives. Such instances in the Scriptures and in the lives of others teach us how to regain in quiet what we've lost in the hustle and bustle of our intensely urban, highly industrialized and technologically complex culture.

MAKING TIME FOR SOLITUDE

Finding times for solitude definitely requires our making a choice.

A friend of mine, a businessman who lives in the Northwest, recently told me of his experience. An almost vicious combination of factors was pressing in on him: difficulty with one of his kids, a vocational decision and other professional pressures. He wasn't really anxious to run from any of these situations, but he did want to know God's will and His way for dealing with each of them.

So, he spoke with his wife, and in the midst of this convergence of difficulty, he explained to her his sense of "being called away" for a few days. He asked, "Would it be okay with you, Honey?"

Her sensitive response? "Okay, go for it."

My friend felt God was calling him to take three days, so he drove to the coast of Oregon, about 100 miles from where he lived in the Willamette Valley, and he found a place to be alone with God. And there in a condo on the beach, he spent three days fasting, reading the Bible and writing in a journal the things God unfolded to his heart as the Lord began to unravel tension and unveil direction.

"That was all I did, Jack," he said. "I read the Word and spent time with God. I have no way to tell you what happened! It was life-transforming. Quiet walks and talks on the beach became releasing in God's presence. When I came back, I don't know if the son we were having trouble with had changed or if it was my change of perspective on him, but we came out of the woods with that problem. Then, business suddenly rectified itself, while I also soon received perfect clarity on the decision I was to make."

This experience is worth studying for emulation. Alone in solitude, God met a man because the man gave Him time. He didn't only get away to the quiet; he got away to the Lord God.

That's an important point to distinguish when we talk about solitude, reflection or meditation in the life of a Christian disciple. Because the general value of meditation is understood in every tradition—it's promoted by most religious systems and is also a very real part of New Age philosophy—I want to be distinctly clear. When I speak of meditation or solitude, I am not relating it to any context other than *being in the presence of God*.

The Christian disciple's practice of solitude is not about connecting with some inner consciousness or being "at one with the universe." Such mystical or psychological self-help systems can lead a person to make himself available to abstract "energies" and end up conjuring demonic confusion. But a Christian in prayerful solitude isn't seeking an abstract contact with "the infinite"; we're seeking *Jesus*.

Those meddling in an undefined spiritual realm, however sincere their pursuit of life's possibilities may be, can become tragically self-destructive. But what we're discussing has no part in any such order of confusion.

JESUS VISITED ME

I've been greatly blessed in my own experience by the renewing power of solitude. Let me relate a case from my own quest.

I had been ill for a sustained period of weeks. I had still been able to keep my schedule, but the combination of maintaining my pastoral work and speaking schedule, along with the nagging physical drag the affliction had put on my body, had brought me to a devastating point of weakness, weariness and exhaustion. Already in an overextended condition and recognizing that the next several weeks offered little reprieve, my view of the immediate future was becoming very bleak. Expectancy was low, anticipation almost absent. This combination was draining me and begetting an indifference to, rather than a desire for, ministry.

Still, within I felt a longing—a hunger for *something* from God. And that's what prompted my saying to Anna, "Honey, I think I'll go up to the mountains." She replied instantly, yet gently, "You know, when I awoke this morning, I felt that's what you needed. You go ahead. Go early." Her quick response wasn't due to any strain showing on our relationship but rather to her own sensitivity to my stressed condition, which confirmed my need for solitude—for being with the Lord. Alone.

I was due to speak two days later at a college's autumn retreat at a conference center in the San Bernardino Mountains. So rather than continuing to press my schedule at home the next 24 hours before leaving, I arranged to leave early.

I was drained in my soul, exhausted in body and thirsty in spirit.

Upon arrival at the conference center, I did little except *be*— I *did* almost nothing. My time was devoted to simply *being* with Jesus.

How well I recall sitting on the porch of the small mountain cabin. Just sitting. Looking into the brush or up at the pines or beyond to the higher elevations. And I would quietly talk—informally—to the Lord. I would weep as I sang, without gusto but with a deep sense of quest, "As the deer panteth for the water, so my soul longeth after Thee."[1] And it was in that setting that *it* happened.

One of the most memorable encounters of my entire life came during the afternoon of that 24-hour period of solitude. In this setting I was shown the sheer love of God. All I can say is *Jesus visited me.*

I don't mean I saw an apparition. Nor am I claiming a trancelike experience. But that day, as I strolled into a grove of magnificent redwoods, quietly expressing my thanks to God for His grace and goodness and patience with me, I was suddenly, powerfully, genuinely and humbly aware of His presence. He made Himself known to me.

Yes, it was emotional. No, it wasn't imaginary. But in a way I will never forget, I was refreshed and reminded how infinitely gentle the love of God is and how fully His presence is available if I will give Him time, by withdrawing from other persons and pressures and just let *Him* be made known to me.

Of course, we can't go to the mountains or the coast every week to have some time for solitude. But let me suggest something that might assist you on an ongoing basis. Allow me to describe how I more commonly include the discipline of solitude in my schedule.

First, it's not something that I mark on my calendar, but it comes when I know it's time. About every week to 10 days, as a general rule, I will find I'm not sleeping well on a given night. I usually do sleep—quite well—but there are times when my mind is restless, usually stirred as I think of things undone or forthcoming, and I'll wake up in the midnight hours.

Now, I can lie there and think, fret, worry or wonder wearily, *When will I go back to sleep?* But instead I get up, put on my bathrobe and go to the living room. Then I just sit in the dark, looking out the window into the night and simply saying to my Lord, "Jesus, I'm just here to be with You."

Does He care? Does God "count" such nonperformance-oriented behavior?

The answer: *Absolutely, yes!*

I don't know the story of your romantic past, but I remember well the early days of Anna's and my relationship and the things that laid the foundation for our fulfilling togetherness to continue for more than three decades now. But we had times even then when just being together and saying very little was more permanently enriching than any verbal or physical expression. And if that value is discoverable and verifiable in a human relationship, make no mistake, friend: Your Lord Jesus is quite happy to have you or me just be with Him, person to person, in His presence and growing to *know* Him.

Look at what God's Word has to say on this theme:

Wait on the LORD; be of good courage, and He shall strengthen your heart; wait, I say, on the LORD! (Ps. 27:14).

I wait for the LORD, my soul waits, and in His word I do hope. My soul waits for the Lord (Ps. 130:5,6).

There is also a touching verse in the Psalms that refers to the animals:

These all wait for You, that You may give them their food in due season (Ps. 104:27).

Years ago, in *Waiting on God,* Andrew Murray wrote tenderly of how this passage shows the way the animal kingdom is attended to by the heavenly Father, faithfully and completely. Yet they contribute absolutely nothing to Him to bring about His tender response and care. They simply wait on Him. Likewise, we all need to be renewed, and Jesus Himself told us the Creator certainly cares no less for us:

Therefore I say to you, do not worry about your life, what you will eat or what you will drink; nor about your body, what you will put on. Is not life more than food and the body more than clothing? Look at the birds of the air, for they neither sow nor reap nor gather into

barns; yet your heavenly Father feeds them. Are you not
of more value than they?

Which of you by worrying can add one cubit to his
stature? So why do you worry about clothing? Consider
the lilies of the field, how they grow: they neither toil nor
spin; and yet I say to you that even Solomon in all his
glory was not arrayed like one of these.

Now if God so clothes the grass of the field, which
today is, and tomorrow is thrown into the oven, will He
not much more clothe you, O you of little faith?
Therefore do not worry, saying, "What shall we eat?" or
"What shall we drink?" or "What shall we wear?" For
after all these things the Gentiles seek. For your heavenly Father knows that you need all these things.

But seek first the kingdom of God and His righteousness, and all these things shall be added to you.
Therefore do not worry about tomorrow, for tomorrow
will worry about its own things. Sufficient for the day is
its own trouble (Matt. 6:25-34).

Listen, loved one. Jesus is saying the same to us today:

> *Why do you let yourself be pressed by the matters of*
> *tomorrow? Why do you try to figure out how you're going*
> *to work it all out? Can you add a foot and a half to your*
> *height? Then why do you think you can get yourself out of the*
> *hole you are in—out and up from under the pressures*
> *that weigh you down?*

When Jesus says, "Look at the lilies of the field," I don't think
He's only saying, "See how the Father cares for nature." I believe
He may also be addressing our basic need to get out and get

away—to *first* make time to be alone with Him and *then* be reminded by His creation.

As I said, we can't always go to the mountains or coast, but often in the early morning, I simply go outside. Just as at nighttime, alone in the living room, I am with the Lord, there are times when I'll walk through the neighborhood before others are out and active. Other times, I'll just go out into the yard. These can be wonderful moments of solitude.

Not long ago, the Lord touched me as I walked in our backyard, quietly communing with Him. It was early, just past dawn, when He met me in a way that makes me think I understand something of what the writer of the song meant when he said:

I come to the garden alone,
While the dew is still on the roses;
And the voice I hear, falling on my ear;
The Son of God discloses.

And He walks with me,
And He talks with me,
And He tells me I am His own.
And the joy we share,
As we tarry there,
None other has ever known.[2]

That hymn is a reminder of how much we need times of solitude—just *being* with God, seeking the kind of relationship that does nothing more than open us up to His love through dependent, childlike *waiting*.

But we live in a world that doesn't sing such songs much anymore. Ours is a world where gardens are fewer, where the environment is being eroded by smog and other forms of pollution. And simultaneously, it seems, souls are being eroded by the force and flow of duty's daily demands and corroded by the pressure-filled atmosphere of self-inflicted and externally required circumstance. So the simplicity and beauty that come by just being with the Lord have become difficult-to-find commodities. But, loved one, solitude *can* be found, even in "waiting" at a desk.

Solitude and Journaling

Let me introduce you to the powerful potential of times of solitude involving the companion disciplines of reflection and journaling. This aspect of being quiet before God is a dynamic that has helped multitudes in every era, but I think it is especially needed today to maintain sanity in a sometimes wild and weird world.

Look at Philippians 4:8,9 with me:

> Finally, brethren, whatever things are true, whatever things are noble, whatever things are just, whatever things are pure, whatever things are lovely, whatever things are of good report, if there is any virtue and if there is anything praiseworthy—meditate on these things. The things which you learned and received and heard and saw in me, these do, and the God of peace will be with you.

I think these words point to reflection in times of quiet *with* God, just as the two prior verses (see vv. 6,7) point to supplication in times of prayer *before* God. The anxiety release of impassioned, binding-and-loosing supplication is wisely to be complemented by our quiet, pensive thinking on God's goodness.

Logizo, the Greek verb for "think on these things," is a mathematical or bookkeeping term. It points toward reflection as a means to take time and tally the goodnesses of God—*keeping score of the good things!* Why? Because we so easily become preoccupied with things that aren't so good. We need to think on the lovely and the blessed and the beauty of God's acts of kindness, mercy and provision.

I've also found it's wise to write down the bad things I am currently facing or being troubled by. If I write my problems down on paper, amazingly, I always find two things to be true. First, there weren't as many as I had thought. Second, when I write them down before the Lord, it seems as though the mere act of writing before Him both shrinks the threat of my problems and starts their solution. Right then, I will begin to sense direction and experience peace. There's something about defining those monsters on paper that moves them out of the fog of confusion and turmoil. Writing them in the presence of Jesus gives perspective on *their* true size—and *His!* There's great power released through reflection and meditation in Christ's presence. Give time to it.

HOW TO JOURNAL

When you journal, you simply write down things that occur to you when you're alone with the Lord. They don't have to be poetic or profound. But you do need to have a special place where you write these things.

You don't need a fancy journal. A simple ringed binder can work very well. I often use a plain pad of yellow paper with lines on it. Though I have nicer journals, this very unimpressive pad serves me best, it seems.

What, then, shall you journal?

Journaling can involve self-examination, interaction with God's Word and simply recording what you hear the Lord speak to your soul.

Self-Examination

I don't mean you should dredge up the past in an effort to convince God that you're now holier because you're feeling more guilty than ever. Still, the Bible shows the importance of coming before the Lord to let our hearts be examined in His presence. This is illustrated in the book of Psalms, the greatest "journal" in history. So many of the psalms are simply the product of people who wrote in the presence of God, describing their fears, their failures and their faith.

In Psalm 38, David responds to the chastening and correcting of God by writing down his thoughts.

In Psalm 51, David writes of his confession of sin before the Lord.

Quiet, then, as I have said, is the first step in our sanctification.

**ST. BASIL
THE GREAT**
BISHOP OF CAESAREA
330-379

In Psalm 73, the psalmist complains before God about how discouraged he is about how well those who hate God are prospering. Think of that. A man frankly, boldly says, "God, I'm not doing well, and it bothers me that the people who don't seem to care anything about You appear to be doing so much better!"

Ever feel that way? David did, too.

God not only isn't threatened by such heart cries, but when David did it, God even decided to put it in His Big Journal—the eternal Word of the holy Scriptures!

But there's a reason: David's *registering* discouragement didn't *result* in discouragement. In that same psalm, after logging his discontent and his complaint, David ends by saying, "This is the sourness of soul I felt *until I came into the presence of the Lord*" (see Ps. 73:16,17,21-28). It's a beautiful, powerful and pivotal point. And that same transition will happen when we get alone with Him and take time to examine our hearts honestly before God.

Interaction with the Word

Journaling may include writing down my subjective response to what I have read in my devotional use of the Bible. I don't mean the fruit of my study so much as my lessons of *discovery* when I'm alone with the Lord and His Word.

In Psalm 19, David describes the preciousness of the Word to him and expresses his delight in it:

> More to be desired are [Your commandments] than gold, yea, than much fine gold; sweeter also than honey and the honeycomb. Moreover by them Your servant is warned, and in keeping them there is great reward (Ps. 19:10,11).

That's a journaled expression of thanks for God's laws. Then David writes his response to the Word, having reflected on it and its intent toward him:

> Cleanse me from secret faults. Keep back Your servant also from presumptuous sins; let them not have dominion over me. Then I shall be blameless, and I shall be innocent of great transgression. Let the words of my mouth and the meditation of my heart be acceptable in Your sight, O LORD, my strength and my redeemer (Ps. 19:12-14).

All of Psalm 119 is very similar, in that the author is saying, "Lord, this is what Your Word means to me." It's more than honoring the Word of God as the "whole counsel of God" (Acts 20:27); it also exemplifies our personal response to the things He says from His Word to *us*—as we listen to the Lord speaking to us when we humble our hearts before His open Book.

The Holy Spirit's Dealings

In the atmosphere of solitude the Holy Spirit will often speak to us. He has always done that, and He does that still today. Personally. And when He does, it's good to journal it.

> When You said, "Seek My face," my heart said to You, "Your face, LORD, I will seek" (Ps. 27:8).

Can you see it? The Holy Spirit spoke to the psalmist's heart; he recognized it and wrote his response: "Lord, what You're saying to me by Your Spirit, I say back to You now. I'm going to do it."

I recently came across this thought: *A person's spirituality is the sum of their responses to what they believe to be the voice of God.* That's a good definition of spiritual growth: tuning to what the Lord says to you and then responding on His terms. You'll find it happens best when you have sufficient time alone with Him to hear His voice, to record His words to you and to live as His Holy Spirit directs, refreshes, corrects and renews.

I've learned to read in the discipline of solitude and to depend on the renewal it can bring. I've also found great help from the discipline of journaling God's dealings with my heart.

These practices converged in an account I journaled and then incorporated a couple of years ago in one of my books. *Moments with Majesty* is a compilation of about a hundred short articles, most of which were written in times when I was alone with God and He would breathe a concept to my understanding or clarify a viewpoint in my mind. In one of these articles, I tell a story about one of the most pressured occasions in my life and a time of solitude worked for me by God's grace.

Remembering Jade Cove

Anna and I were recently coming back from Carmel, where we celebrated our wedding anniversary. Driving south on Highway 1, that famous roadway that hugs the Pacific Coast, I reminisced as we passed Jade Cove, near Big Sur. That's the place where, years ago, by the grace of God, I "turned the corner." I don't mean a curve on that twisting, perilous highway, but the turnaround at Jade Cove rescued me from something as bad as a car accident.

For several weeks I had been experiencing a horrible accumulation of pressure—mental and emotional. Work had piled up, schedule demands were burning me out. Through a combination of circumstances, I was riding the ragged edge of a nervous breakdown.

Some nights I would dream of being chased—and then crushed—by a massive object relentlessly pursuing and slowly gaining on me as I ran to escape it. Other nights I feared closing my eyes to go to sleep, feeling if I did I would not awaken again—that my heart would stop or my breath cease. I was rational enough to know this wasn't true but weak enough in my emotionally drained condition that I was unable to break the tormenting thoughts.

Then I discovered the words of the songwriter. Listen:

> I will both lie down in peace, and sleep; for You alone, O LORD, make me dwell in safety (Ps. 4:8).

And another lyric:

> I lay down and slept; I awoke, for the LORD sustained me (Ps. 3:5).

I can hardly describe the power of those words as they flowed across my weary soul. I grasped them for the reliable, eternal words of truth that they are. They were all the more meaningful to me when I remembered they were written by a very busy man—a man of accomplishment and crushing responsibilities. David was a successful king and a conquering hero, yet a man who needed release from pressures that threatened his sleep.

God's words buoyed my soul for several weeks, sustaining me until that day on Highway 1. I was driving slowly northward, hoping a break in schedule and a change of scene would take the cascading voices off my mind and the rising fear from my heart.

I had stopped at the sign. Jade Cove, it read. I went down near the water's edge to look at the beautiful seascape. To listen to the waves. To feel the sea spray on my face. To pray.

It was there something happened—better yet, Someone. Because as surely as I knew His Word had sustained me when fear plagued my nights, I knew God's presence had drawn near to deliver my mind. Like fog burning off the coastline, the Son of God simply reached down and lifted the burden I had carried for months.

I share that with you now to urge *you* to receive His Word: "I will both lie down in peace, and sleep; for You alone, O LORD, make me dwell in safety."

Call upon His Holy Spirit to deliver you. I know He will, because He did that for me at a place called Jade Cove, and He did it through the power of a man named Jesus.

He's there for you. Right now. You don't even have to go to Jade Cove, because . . .

Whoever calls on the name of the Lord shall be saved (Acts 2:21).[3]

ON WRITING YOUR OWN BOOK

It was the beloved Esther Kerr Rusthoi who coined that phrase, minting it in my consciousness in a priceless way several years ago. It was her way of exhorting believers to "hear what the Holy Spirit is saying to the Church"—or more specifically, to you.

To those who refuse to acknowledge a personal God, the suggestion that a loving Father speaks to His children is mocked as mere fantasy. To those ignorant of the Lord Jesus' constant ministry as Head of the Body of His Church, directing the activity of the members of that Body, such communication is considered unnecessary. To those who resist the tender voice of the Holy Spirit's prompting, impressing, balancing and prodding forward, such "whispers" are labeled fanaticism.

Eli's counsel to young Samuel is still practical wisdom to those who are just beginning to learn to hear the voice of God: "Say, 'Speak, LORD, for Your servant hears'" (1 Sam. 3:9).

Isaiah's prophecy forecasts a way of fruitfulness born from obedience: "Your ears shall hear a word behind you, saying, 'This is the way, walk in it'" (Isa. 30:21).

Jesus not only taught that sheep will know the Shepherd's voice, but He declared, "My sheep hear My voice . . . and they follow Me" (John 10:27). He asserted that receiving His Word—responding to it—is every bit as essential as recognizing it.

The kind of listening each of these passages describes is that which brings appropriate action. It is the simple and trusting response of a child, as in Samuel's case, or the sensitive and discerning response of a maturing learner, which Isaiah speaks about.

In describing the shepherd/sheep relationship as the basis for this order of hearing, He is saying (1) if you don't listen, you won't know where He's going, and (2) if you don't respond, you won't be very close to where He is.

In other words, everything is at stake: His guidance and His glory. Without listening carefully, we can miss both.

Friends, I hear a voice.

I think you do, too.

It sometimes calls, sometimes corrects, sometimes commands, sometimes directs, sometimes enthralls, sometimes teaches, sometimes demands and sometimes reaches . . .

. . . to touch the ear again with a loving, "Follow Me."

Listen.[3]

Into the community you were called—the call was not meant for you alone; in the community of the called you bear your cross, you struggle, you pray. You are not alone even in death, and on the Last Day you will be only one of the great congregation of Jesus Christ. If you scorn the fellowship of the brethren, you reject the call of Jesus Christ.

DIETRICH BONHOEFFER, 1906-1945

———∞———

PRINCIPLE

Worship is the ultimate priority of every believer, not only because God is worthy of our worship but also because it is His designed means to arrange His entry into our personal world and into those circumstances where His sovereign workings have placed us. Worship is the capstone to the 10 primary disciplines, because it opens the doorway to God's superintendency and supernatural presence and power as the governing influences and purifying elements in all life issues. Worship is also the pathway into prayer—the all-encompassing discipline—and is prayer's essential point of entry to the Father and of faith in His almightiness.

———∞———

PRACTICE

Walk with me through the most basic ideas about worship—from the importance of gathering with others in assembly to the power of learning life's pathway of progress through the building of private altars, as season follows season in our growth. We will find that the practice and discipline of worship is the starting place for all of life in Christ, for it determines to whom we yield and what we will prioritize. Wholehearted worship is essential to retaining childlikeness in spirit and Christlikeness in character, both of which flow from a constantly renewed humility before God's presence and are sustained by the river of joy and life that flows from His throne.

LIVING AS A WORSHIPER

But the hour is coming, and now is, when the true worshipers will worship the Father in spirit and truth; for the Father is seeking such to worship Him.

JOHN 4:23

There is a global worship awakening in progress! Everywhere we look today the Body of Christ is coming alive in new dimensions of vibrant worship. Without disrespect toward Church history or tradition, a fullness of freedom can today be found in almost every sector of the Body.

There are some places where this newness is seen and understood only in musical terms, as though contemporary song were the very definition of worship renewal. In other areas, the renewal is further defined by physical departures—guitars and drums in place of organs, worship singers rather than robed choirs, projected lyrics in lieu of hymnals and expressive exuberance instead of dignified reserve. But this is not what true renewal in worship is all about.

An awakening to worship becomes transient where only surface changes are applied. There are far deeper issues—two primary ones—and it is the part of a disciple to understand, respond and pursue worship in the light of these substantial issues that bring depth and durability to worship.

The first issue in worship is our focus—*whom* we worship. To read the "worship handbook" given us in the Bible is to become riveted on this fact: The psalms are all about a mighty and wondrous God, and yet they breathe with such intimacy! The psalmists' candor and freedom, their awe and amazement, the forthrightness of their complaints and the joyfulness of their praise all work together to show the almighty, eternal, omnipotent Creator being approached with warmth, humility, happiness, abandonment and reverence. In each psalm, we see a human being boldly entering God's presence, understanding that He is welcomed there. And the worshiper is clearly active, not merely pensive. He is singing, shouting, bowing, kneeling, lifting hands and dancing with head bowed and head upraised, silent one moment and exuberant the next! *Worship that has found the throne of the living God cannot be anything but alive. Transcending intellectual analysis, it overflows with joy as the human heart comes in contact with its Creator and Redeemer.*

The second issue in worship is its purpose—*why* we worship. For some, this overlaps the first issue already discussed. *Why?* is answered with *Because God is worthy of our worship*, and of course this is true. But I want to deal with the reason God Himself has called us to worship and has given us the privilege of worshiping Him. Make no mistake—He has a plan for it. His plan was most concisely enunciated when He commanded the Tabernacle to be built, saying, "Make a place where I may dwell among you. There I will meet with you, and I will speak with you" (see Exod. 25:8-22). His designed purpose for worship is still the same: *Worship is both the means by which we may enter the presence of God and the means by which He is welcomed into the midst of our world.* The teaching of Jesus notes this, calling for worship in prayer: "Our Father in heaven, hallowed (Holy, Holy!) be Your name (for there is none like You in Your greatness and glory)" (Matt. 6:9). His prayer then immediately proceeds to invite God into our present circumstances: "Your kingdom come (its power and glory). Your will be done (execute Your Word here) on earth (where my world needs Your presence, power and works) as it is in heaven (for an invasion of the heavenly is needed where I live, O Lord!)" (v. 10).

The discipline of worship calls each of us to understand the power of praise: Worship is a means of invoking the presence of God's throne—here in the joy, pain, hurt or hope of my present moment.

> But thou art holy, O thou that inhabitest the praises of Israel (Ps. 22:3, *KJV*).

The wonder of those words is wrapped in the richness of the verb "inhabit," which literally translates in this text to read, "You are *enthroned* upon the praises!"

The discipline of worship is part of a life that expands in knowing God, His power and His blessing. This discipline finds many expressions, from private praise to worshiping with the assembly, from singing with gladness to giving with sacrifice. But at the center of it all is a dynamic each disciple must come to realize: *My praise and worship will determine the dimensions of my forward advancement along the pathway of discipleship. I will advance no further than my heart of worship allows me. I may become deep in knowledge and brilliant in spiritual insights, but my worship before God will determine my true stature as a son or daughter and my maturity as a growing servant-disciple.*

The following are a few words prompted by the Holy Spirit and given to our congregation over the years. They are on the theme "Praise Is Your Pathway":

> Periodically, over the years, the Lord has pressed specific points upon us—points of truth He seeks us to acknowledge in the ongoing pattern of life. It is to these we turn, as to milestone markers.

Has praise been a hallmark of your life? Has praise been your constant practice? Has your understanding of praise and its role in your life been growing with the passing months and years?

A few basic reminders from Scripture can bring your life back on track . . .

From Acts 16: Darkness surrounds this hour as it did Paul and Silas in the Philippian prison. Their praise brought God's hand by an earthquake, and out of the night a hopeless jailer was saved. Now, let your praises rise! As you praise continually, spiritual shock waves go out into the world around you. It will bring your release and the release of many into the kingdom of God.

From Psalm 26: Praise is your pathway through the mired circumstances of the present world. Your step will be uncertain and slide, unless you recognize that your praises form stepping stones by which the Father paves your way into the future purpose He has for you.

From Job 38: As the morning stars sang His praise at creation, accompanying His great display of power with their worship, let your voices join with the heavenly song. Praise the Lord. Sing unto the Lord. Sing with your spirit and sing with your understanding; for as you sing praises unto Him, He continues His great creative working . . . and in your midst you shall see the marvelous works of God, the Lord of the new creation.

"Let's just praise the Lord," one writer has proposed, and some might suggest this is a rather closed view of things. I disagree. It's the open door to everything, and the pathway God directs us to walk into the "every-things" of His best will and purpose for each of us.[1]

ASSEMBLE YOURSELVES TOGETHER

When we talk about the ever-expanding life of the disciple walking with Christ, we cannot help but come face-to-face with the fundamental personal discipline of worship (1) *daily*, as a private devotional practice and (2) *regularly* assembling together with the people of God in a local congregation.

I realize I might be suspect on the second point, having spent most of my life as pastor of a church. Some may be thinking, *Of course a pastor would say that. After all, he needs people in attendance or he's out of a job!* But the gathering of the people was never man's idea. It was God's:

> From everyone who gives it willingly with his heart you shall take My offering. . . . And let them make Me a sanctuary, that I may dwell among them. . . . And there I will meet with you, and I will speak with you from above the mercy seat (Exod. 25:2,8,22).

You see, the divine idea of assembly has nothing to do with keeping attendance records, or increasing the size of a local congregation or swelling a church's coffers. The issue is that the living God wants to meet with His people as a corporate body, as well as in private fellowship.

The practice of worship with the assembly of saints is a gathering together that is pointedly and prophetically directed. We have already dealt with worship at a private level, but in the Word of God worship is called forth (1) in assembly, (2) at appointed times, (3) in faithfulness to God's Word and (4) as a discipline of the believer. "Get Me to the Church on Time" might well be a theme for each of us.

Of course, the flesh has counterarguments to challenge the discipline's call:

Perhaps I need a break. I don't want to let religious tradition push me to performance. If my heart's not in it, there's no use going—and I just don't "feel it" today. It's probably more honest of me to stay home. God won't mind, especially since I'm being more honest by not going than if I went feeling like this.

I'm so beat today. I'd be a hindrance to others if I go. My tired presence would only siphon off the jubilation of the assembly. How could I possibly receive something from God in my condition?

We had such a fight last night, and I still have such a rotten attitude. How could God take my presence seriously or want to speak to me?

I have fumbled so miserably this week that if I go to church today, God will see me as a hypocrite, like I was trying to fake Him into thinking I'm a good guy just because I showed up at His place. I better get my act cleaned up before I go. Maybe I'll just stay home and pray—read the Word, show Him I'm sincere. Yeah. Next week I'll be better.

Ever hear your own "small voice" arguing this way? Silence it, because God's Word has an overarching answer to every claim the flesh makes. If you're tired, stumbling, fumbling or needful, He says, "Okay. Assemble. For it's in the environment of your obedience and in the presence of My people that I'll be able to best deal with you—to refresh you, to renew you or to restore you!"

THE APPROACHING DAY

Not forsaking the assembling of ourselves together, as is the manner of some, but exhorting one another, and so much the more as you see the Day approaching (Heb. 10:25).

This text from the book of Hebrews expresses two very sobering thoughts. First, this was a discipline problem in the Early Church. *What? You mean people neglected church attendance back then?* Clearly, yes. But a second, more sobering issue than missing church is noted in these words: "so much the more as you see the Day approaching."

Listen. The command to assemble is cast in terms that indicate the truth that there is power in the discipline of worship. The discipline of corporate worship protects against giving in to the spirit of the times (see Rom. 12:1,2), losing touch with the spirit of anticipation of Jesus' return (see 1 Tim. 4:8; 2 Tim. 4:8) and neglecting our role as stewards of gifts for which we'll be accountable when He comes (see Matt. 25:14-30).

The expression "the Day approaching," of course, refers to the second coming of our Lord Jesus Christ. Those of sound-minded faith know that any day in our lifetime is as likely a day as any for His return, and they live accordingly: "Lord, when You come, You'll find me faithful. At Your appearing You'll find me *ready!*"

Don't mistake my words. I'm not suggesting something so biblically insipid as the notion that if you're not in church when Jesus comes, you'll miss the Rapture! That isn't the issue. But neither can you and I escape all the implications of the idea that the

Day is approaching. It's simply a matter of raw obedience to God and His Word. Go to church! Dash the notions that assembling with the Body is only ritual or tradition. You need to be there!

C. S. Lewis's *Screwtape Letters* examines the devious ways of subtle, satanic spirits—the way whispering ideas creep into our minds, selling notions that seem so momentarily logical, such as *The church is only a historic, institutional, traditional, man-concocted idea, and going every week is a human invention!* or *The church I attend is so "dead," so boorish!*

But such dead thoughts need to be identified as coming from the Death Pit itself. There is *nothing* dead about you and me making a habit of being there. When an honest soul humbles itself and comes to meet Him, Jesus then can make Himself alive to us *anywhere.*

Come. Sing. Love. Give. Listen. Don't criticize. Smile. Praise. Look past imperfect people to God. Worship Him. Stop analyzing the limited skills of others. Humble your heart.

If you open yourself to His love, being willing to be faithful in church attendance, you'll find His reward.

It's worthwhile to look at Jesus' own habits in this regard. Read Luke 4:16, which speaks of Jesus' custom of regular "church attendance":

> So He came to Nazareth, where He had been brought up.
> And as His custom was, He went into the synagogue on
> the Sabbath Day, and stood up to read.

I can't help laughing, in a sense, at any critic of church attendance who refuses to go on the grounds that the place is too spiritually "dead"!

You want to argue church attendance with Jesus? Go ahead, do it!

"Well, Lord, You certainly know that things aren't as spiritual as they ought to be. You know the people there aren't warm, understanding or friendly!"

Jesus replies, "Warm and friendly? Have you ever been in Nazareth? The day I was there they tried to throw Me off the cliff!" But Jesus showed up anyway, *as was His custom!*

Case closed.

First Corinthians 16:2 shows us the pattern of life in the Early Church, further indicating a continuing discipline of church gatherings:

> On the first day of the week let each one of you lay something aside, storing up as he may prosper, that there be no collections when I come.

Hear it? When you meet together "on the first day of the week." Our Sunday appointment isn't anything to be argued and debated. Let's never belabor the issue of *Which day?* If anyone worships any other day, I certainly don't mind; but there's no arguing *against* Sunday.

> One person esteems one day above another; another esteems every day alike. Let each be fully convinced in his own mind. He who observes the day, observes it to the Lord; and he who does not observe the day, to the Lord he does not observe it (Rom. 14:5,6).

The real issue is that on *some day*, each week, you gather with the saints.

The biblical evidence shows that the Early Church gathered on Sunday. And don't accept the argument that these believers had submitted to a dead pagan tradition that bound them to some kind of a carnality, or pagan aberration, resulting in Sunday worship. No, sir! They worshiped on Sunday, because they recognized it as the day Jesus rose from the dead. Every weekly assembly was a celebration of the resurrection life of Christ!

So, let's continue that ongoing recelebrating in our obedience to worship at a weekly appointed time. Here are four reasons:

1. We will find that grace is released to us, because we make room for that grace through our obedience and acceptance of the discipline of attendance.

2. It gives us a chance to acknowledge with humility, *I need the Body of Christ.* We need to be with the local body because we are members of a living Body, and the "member" separated from its body will decay.

3. We acknowledge a distinct accountability to the Body of Christ, we show a practical availability to serve, and we allow a place and time for correction. We show up, and by our presence, thereby acknowledge we're righteously submitted to Christ's rule in, and through, His Church.

4. We manifest a model: "In all things showing yourself to be a pattern of good works" (Titus 2:7). By worshiping together at an appointed time, we show a pathway for others to observe—not as a self-righteous display, but rather as a demonstration of the Lord's way.

WORSHIP AT AN ALTAR

We have seen that there is wisdom in our obedience to live as worshipers who acknowledge an appointed time. Let us now consider worship as a time for meeting with God.

We need to come regularly into the presence of God in worship, to encounter Him through worship. We have, as I've sometimes put it, an unalterable need of an altar.

This aspect of worship often happens best when we're alone with the Lord, although it is not a substitute for our attendance at church. The Bible doesn't give us that option. Both public and private times of worship are needed in a disciple's life with Christ. Along with our gathering times with the church, let's also have times when we meet the Lord at private altars of worship—times of personal encounter and growth.

God's Word provides examples of this in the many altars found in the life of Abraham. After the Lord called Abraham (still called Abram at this point), He made it clear that the man's destiny was to realize not only promise for his own life but also promise for many lives that would touch the nations. There is no way to determine exactly how all this distilled in Abraham's soul. At the very least, he had to have felt that he was called to something well beyond his capacity to fulfill—unless God were to help him.

If we trace Abraham's life, we will discover several "altar moments"—at least eight pivotal events at which he encountered the Lord in distinct ways. The following four are most illustrative for our purposes:

1. The Altar of Promise

The first altar moment involves two dynamics directly related to our experiences:

> Then Abram took Sarai his wife and Lot his brother's
> son, and all their possessions that they had gathered,
> and the people whom they had acquired in Haran, and

I glorify Thee through the eternal and heavenly High Priest, Jesus Christ, Thy beloved Son, through whom be glory to Thee with Him and the Holy Spirit, both now and for the ages to come. Amen.

POLYCARP
BISHOP OF SMYRNA
69-155(?)

they departed to go to the land of Canaan. So they came to the land of Canaan. Abram passed through the land to the place of Shechem, as far as the terebinth tree of Moreh. And the Canaanites were then in the land. Then the LORD appeared to Abram and said, "To your descendants I will give this land." And there he built an altar to the LORD, who had appeared to him (Gen. 12:5-7).

God said, "To your descendants I will give this land," and there Abraham built an altar to the Lord. It is an altar of promise, but it is also an altar amid adversaries. The picture is focused: This is a classic snapshot of God's declared purpose in our lives, in immediate juxtaposition to the adversary's presence and potential to inhibit that promise from being fulfilled.

Take that thought and apply it to your own life. What promises has God made alive to your heart? What potential has He indicated He intends to multiply and prosper through you? And in contrast, have you found obstacles, opposition and oppression? Of course you have. The answer is to *seal* the promise at God's altar, securing it in faith. What is fixed in place at an altar with God will find solidity when it later comes under attack. The adversary's resistance is real, but what is sealed at the Father's throne will survive and triumph:

> For this reason I also suffer these things; nevertheless I am not ashamed, for I know whom I have believed and am persuaded that He is able to keep what I have committed to Him until that Day (2 Tim. 1:12).

2. The Altar of Intimacy

Abraham's second altar is equally demonstrative of a stabilizing step in faith's progress. It took place at an altar of increased familiarity, of growth in intimacy:

> And he moved from there to the mountain east of Bethel, and he pitched his tent with Bethel on the west and Ai on the east; there he built an altar to the LORD and called on the name of the LORD (Gen. 12:8).

Abraham's calling on the *name* of the Lord is a direct reference to a distinct dimensional grasp of something more of the Lord's nature, character and fullness of person. The Bible speaks of His name as more than merely a title or label:

> The name of the LORD is a strong tower; the righteous run to it and are safe (Prov. 18:10).

Abraham was coming to know the Lord as more than merely the God of all creation and power. He was finding a more intimate familiarity with the Lord and His readiness to meet us in a personally caring, sustaining friendship.

Receiving God's promise for our lives and power over the adversary is not a substitute for growing in intimacy with Him on a personal level. Abraham's faith was not the fruit of formulas and slogans. It was born of a growing relationship at a personal level with the sustaining, personally caring One.

3. The Altar of No Return

Genesis 13:3,4 is a moving testimony to God's grace in retrieving us from the subtle snares of confusion by which even the most faithful of us will sometimes be set back:

> And he went on his journey from the South as far as Bethel, to the place where his tent had been at the beginning, between Bethel and Ai, to the place of the altar which he had made there at first. And there Abram called on the name of the LORD.

Abraham had made a trip to Egypt. Why? We're not told. The Lord had promised him the land where he was, and he was growing in a closer personal knowledge of the Lord—but then he took the trip to Egypt.

Except for the marvelous grace of God, the trip was a sad commentary on Abraham's fear and weakness. But the Lord retrieved him through a show of intervening mercy (see Gen. 12:10-20). And when it was over, Abraham had not only come *through*, but he had also come *out*—magnificently!

This is an altar of no return. It's the time and place where Abraham puts down a stake, saying, "I'm here where God means for me to be, and there will be no wandering ever again!" It's an altar all of us must come to at some point. Our arrival there doesn't mean there will never again be trials, tests or even stumbling. But once the stake is driven, once the altar of no return is built in God's presence, something will transpire in the soul that causes you never again to leave the assigned purposes of God ("this is your land")—to never again drift away in pursuit of anything of other interest or human speculation.

- It needs to happen in the disciple's belief: *Doubt will never again be given a place to question God's will and purpose for me.*
- It needs to happen in the disciple's sense of mission: *I know what God wants me to do; and I'm not only going to do nothing less, but I have come to know I'm good for nothing else!*
- It needs to happen in the disciple's marriage: *There is no other one for me; God has given me one partner for my one lifetime!*

Apply the principle wherever it needs to be applied. Build *your* altar(s) of no return!

4. The Altar of Possession

Abraham had been given the promise that the land would be his, but then the Lord calls him to actually pace it off—to measure the dimensions of God's promise.

Arise, walk in the land through its length and its width, for I give it to you. Then Abram moved his tent, and went and dwelt by the terebinth trees of Mamre, which

are in Hebron, and built an altar there to the LORD (Gen.
13:17,18).

Through this altar of possession Abraham comes to real and
practical terms with a general-until-now promise. It is one thing
to have a given promise and another to have a *possessed* promise.
Abraham's actually walking through the land is evidence of
God's practical ways of bringing any of us to terms with the
details of His will.

Imagination is a wonderful thing; when God captures our
imaginations with His promises, a vision may well become our
treasured hope. But there comes a time when the Lord will bring
us to the reality of the promise—its dimensions and its
demands—when we fully realize all the promise entails. So it is
that He will bring us to an altar at which we (1) confirm our
acceptance of the *implications* of the promise and (2) commit our
life to the *pursuit* of the promise's full outworking.

Such altars are essential. And as we trace the life of faith's
father, we learn the potential that flows from a life of private
worship—walking with God in the secret places of encounter
and growth and coming to know Him in ever-expanding intimacy and ever-broadening mission. Abraham's building of altars is
laden with lessons for us. The unalterable need of an altar is for
learning the wisdom of bringing life's difficult things and turning them into stepping-stones of worship presented before God.

Hebrews 13:10 says we have an altar unlike any other altar,
referring to what we have through the New Covenant: a means
of intimately approaching the living God. It affords a boldness
of access, for we do not have a High Priest who cannot be
touched with our feelings of weakness; instead, He is sensitive to
all we feel. He readily hears us and invites us, "Come boldly to
the throne of grace" (Heb. 4:16).

A classic hymn asks, "Is Your All on the Altar?"

You have longed for sweet peace, and for faith to increase,
And have earnestly, fervently prayed;
But you cannot have rest or be perfectly blest,
Until all on the altar is laid.

Would you walk with the Lord in the light of His Word,
And have peace and contentment always;
You must do His sweet will to be free from all ill,
On the altar your all you must lay.

Oh, we never can know what the Lord will bestow
Of the blessings for which we have prayed,
Till our body and soul He doth fully control,
And our all on the altar is laid.

Who can tell all the love He will send from above,
And how happy our hearts will be made,
Of the fellowship sweet we shall share at His feet,
When our all on the altar is laid.

Refrain:
Is your all on the altar of sacrifice laid?
Your heart, does the Spirit control?
You can only be blest and have peace and sweet rest,
As you yield Him your body and soul.[2]

The summons of this hymn is a healthy reminder for us. As you think of the disciplines of worship, always remember they not only involve high ecstasy and joyous praise in public assembly, but they also call us to plain, private moments of simply being with God. We are also reminded that in every circumstance, especially when hard times come, we should build an altar of life's rock-hard circumstances—and meet God there.

WORSHIP AND STEWARDSHIP

Finally, let me mention one other thing about worship: Worship also involves the stewardship of what God has blessed us with materially.

The Bible makes very clear that the giving of tithes and the bringing of offerings are not simply Old Covenant propositions. I realize that any Bible teacher is vulnerable to criticism when he or she teaches the contemporary practice of tithes and offerings.

I've heard the arguments—every one and from every aspect. And I don't want to seem contentious or obstinate. But let me simply mention two things in answer to such arguments.

First, 2 Corinthians 3 summarily teaches that the glory of the New Covenant will always exceed the glory of the Old. Then if the practice of tithing was designated for God's people in the Old Testament, how can a New Testament believer do less? Answer: We can't, if we grasp the spirit of New Testament giving.

"Well," someone says, "I'll accept that, but I'm not going to call it a tithe." Fine. That's all right. But let the principle be understood, that the giving patterns of the New Covenant can't retreat to less than what was practiced under the Old Covenant—not because we are saved by it, but rather because our stewardship in worship and giving should manifest the spirit of the New Testament which transcends the Old.

Second, Jesus confirmed and approved the practice of tithing. In Matthew 23:23, He faulted the Pharisees for their attentiveness to the smallest detail of tithing, while being inattentive to the great issues of love, justice and graciousness. He ridiculed them, almost fiercely, for their smallness of soul in overlooking great issues of the Law. But in this same verse He went on to say, "These [tithes] you ought to have done, without leaving the others [justice and mercy] undone." Christ clearly approved of tithing, but He also said they should have done *more* than that.

Giving and generosity are taught elsewhere in the Scriptures:

- Paul writes to confirm and approve the generosity of the Philippians (see Phil. 4:10,14-19).
- He calls the Corinthians to liberal giving, notwithstanding hard economic times (see 2 Cor. 8,9).
- Jesus calls us to give: "Give, and it will be given to you: good measure, pressed down, shaken together, and running over will be put into your bosom" (Luke 6:38).

The expression "put into your bosom" refers to clothing that had an apron on the front. Jesus is saying, "You hold that out and it'll hold more than your hand could ever give. God will abound back to you as you learn His way of giving."

I know there are people who take exception and say, "You shouldn't teach, 'Give because God is going to give back.'" But listen, dear one. Let's just face it: We can't get away from the proposition. I admit that ideally the reward He promises would never enter our minds. Nonetheless, if we give, God is going to give back to us. He has built the order of our world; it can't be reversed because it's as much His will as any of His other natural laws. Giving imparts blessing.

It's not even as though God has to make a decision to bless us when we give, as though He watches and says, "Oh, they gave, so now I'll give." No! Rather, the blessing returns because something is released in the invisible realm according to God's reciprocal law of giving. When we live as people who worship Him with faithful stewardship of our finances, there comes a release, an outflowing and overflowing of God's abundance because we have aligned our lives with the order of His ways.

Once you do, you'll find it works. If a person were to leap off a tall building, they wouldn't have to call the law of gravity into action. It just works. And when you come to give, you don't have to call some law of reciprocity into action. It just works. God responds to those who align with His ways, because He has built this gracious response into His system.

As you faithfully worship Him, watch as the grace He gives to you abounds—not because you bought it and not because you earned it, but rather because you have learned obedience. Whether we are gathering together with the saints as a discipline, walking with Him and building altars before and to Him or being faithful in stewardship, we have learned the way of God's people who function in all the facets of worship with obedience, which always has its rich reward.

Part Three

THE
DISCIPLINE OF
PRAYER

*If man is man and God is God, to live without prayer is not merely
an awful thing; it is an infinitely foolish thing.*

PHILLIPS BROOKS
EPISCOPAL BISHOP OF MASSACHUSETTS
1835-1893

*Wherever . . . thou shalt be, pray secretly within thyself. If thou shalt be far
from a house of prayer, give not thyself trouble to seek for one, for thou thyself
art a sanctuary designed for prayer. If thou shalt be in bed, or in any other
place, pray there; thy temple is there.*

ST. BERNARD
ABBOT OF CLAIRVAUX
1091-1153

WALKING THE PATH OF PRAYER

In this manner, therefore, pray: Our Father in heaven, hallowed be Your name. Your kingdom come. Your will be done on earth as it is in heaven. Give us this day our daily bread. And forgive us our debts, as we forgive our debtors. And do not lead us into temptation, but deliver us from the evil one. For Yours is the kingdom and the power and the glory forever. Amen.

MATTHEW 6:9-13

The aged apostle Paul, as he drew his letter to a conclusion, gave a series of short, concise commands summarizing essentials for disciples. There he wrote, "Pray without ceasing" (1 Thess. 5:17).

Whatever else may be said about living as a disciple of Jesus Christ, about walking with Him by faith and in love through trial and in power, clearly prayer is the one discipline above and beneath all others.

I have heard it said that more books have been written on the subject of prayer than on any other worthwhile theme occupying human inquiry or aspiration. Few thinking persons deny there is *something* to this practice. This has often been true even when the person denies there's someone *there* to whom prayer may be offered.

"Prayer" is a word and idea used by the materialist and the Eastern mystic to describe quiet creative reasoning or "transcendent" meditation. Still others characterize prayer as anything from describing a good feeling (toward a cause or person) to an impassioned cry for help from "whoever's out there."

At a fuller, deeper dimension for the disciple of Jesus, prayer is person-to-Person communication—a combination of worship, fellowship and intercession:

- *worship* through adoration, praise and thanksgiving *to* God;
- *fellowship* through devotion, communion and conversation *with* God;
- *intercession* through supplication, fasting and spiritual warfare *before* God.

"Praying always with all prayer and supplication in the Spirit" is a phrase inclusively covering this triad of prayer, as Paul enunciates it in his concluding appeal to the Ephesians (6:18). Some translations read "all *kinds* of prayer," a worthy translation that points us to a learning path of applied growth in understanding the *means* and *methods* of prayer.

The Bible's call to prayer is not a call to the mystical or the theoretical. The pathway of prayer is preeminently learnable. It is not intended to be mysterious, but instead, always practical.

Starting with seven basic steps of prayer as outlined by Jesus when instructing His disciples *how* to pray, we'll conclude with three keys to effective asking *in* prayer and attacking *through* prayer. Throughout we shall move toward applying the one constant the Bible teaches the earnest disciple: "Pray without ceasing."

To learn to live in the spirit of prayer is to learn to walk in the presence of Jesus. Always.

CONFIDENT FAITH

You are all sons of light and sons of the day. We are not of the night nor of darkness.

1 THESSALONIANS 5:5

Nothing is more crippling to effective prayer than not having confidence in our relationship with God. When Jesus refers to God as the Father, He helps us to understand the glorious relationship we are intended to have with Him.

OUR FATHER IN HEAVEN

In this manner, therefore, pray: Our Father in heaven, hallowed be Your name (Matt. 6:9).

Jesus opens His teaching on prayer with an emphasis on our relationship with God as our Father. In doing so, He establishes the foundational truth that we are given grounds for confidence in prayer on the strength of a Father-child relationship, which the Bible says is established and secured through Christ:

Now this is the confidence that we have in Him, that if we ask anything according to His will, He hears us. And if we know that He hears us, whatever we ask, we know that we have the petitions that we have asked of Him (1 John 5:14,15).

Unfortunately, the concept of "father" has been marred for many through disappointing earthly relationships with parents or other authority figures. Because of this all-too-common human fact, Jesus made a point to show us the Father in a way no one else ever could. For in Christ Himself we see that God is a Father who transcends even the finest earthly father; He is able to redeem us from the broken images or painful memories of our lives. As we follow Christ's teachings about the Father and see how He showed us the Father in His life, we come to understand the power of His words to Philip: "He who has seen Me has seen the Father" (John 14:9).

In Luke 15, Jesus uses the story of the prodigal son to paint a magnificent picture of what our Father God is really like. Here is a young man who wasted everything he'd been given—his inheritance, his opportunities and his father's trust. He ended up working in a pigpen in a foreign land. But in unfolding this story, Jesus unveils God's heart toward each of us through five essential phrases. He shows that, regardless of what we have wasted, God's arms are still reaching toward us, openly and lovingly.

The first thing we learn about is God's *quest* for us. The father saw his prodigal son when he was still "a great way off" (v. 20). This shows us something unique and precious about the longing heart of God. As the father watched for his wayward son, so God's heart yearns and watches for each of us, even when we are far away from Him. In other words, regardless of what we have done or where we are, God loves us.

Second, we see that when the father saw the son on his way home, he "had compassion, and ran and fell on his neck and kissed him" (v. 20)—he *received* his son.

I have often reflected on this story, thinking about the reluctance the son must have felt as he drew closer and closer to home. He must have been uneasy about his return, feeling very unworthy. He had squandered his resources, wasted his entire inheritance and had nearly lost his life! He had every reason to doubt that his father would take him back.

But Jesus describes God's open heart toward us by showing how the young man's father welcomed him. The verb tense used here to say "he embraced him and kissed him" is literally translated "he kissed him repeatedly." The father must have received his wandering son with much the same joy that he had when he first embraced the son at his birth. It was as though his son was being born all over again! The father cried, "My son was dead and is alive again; he was lost and is found" (v. 24). And in this same way, it is with joy that God receives us.

Third, after this loving reception, the father called for the finest robe to be given to his son (see v. 22). The particular style of robe referred to was full-length in cut—a garment reserved in those days for one who held a position of honor and prestige. So it is clear that this fallen son was being *restored* to his former posi-

All who call on God in true faith, earnestly from the heart, will certainly be heard, and will receive what they have asked and desired, although not in the hour or in the measure, or the very thing which they ask; yet they will obtain something greater and more glorious than they had dared to ask.

MARTIN LUTHER
1483-1546

tion as an heir in the household. The privileges of relationship with his father were returned to him, even though he had lost the inheritance he'd been given. Likewise, God not only receives us as forgiven sons and daughters, but He also restores us from the losses of our past. Although we may have abandoned the gifts He first gave us, He welcomes us back with a loving embrace and brings us again into our intended place in His will and purposes.

Fourth, the father had a jeweled ring put on his son's finger (see v. 22). How the hearts of those listening to this story for the first time must have leapt when Jesus related this part! They would have recognized instantly the significance of this action, for in ancient times the giving of such a ring indicated the son's full return to partnership with his father in the family's business. The ring gave him the right to exercise authority in all commercial or legal matters, for it represented the full weight of whatever authority or power that family's name carried.

Thus, in calling us to pray "our Father," Jesus shows that God invites us to let Him *authorize us as His partner.* Our prayer in the family name of Jesus is authoritative prayer. And that name is given to us freely and fully, carrying with it all the rights and privileges granted to members of God's eternal family.

Fifth, the father had shoes or sandals placed on his son's feet (see v. 22). These shoes were more than mere clothing. Old Testament imagery teaches that people in mourning or grief commonly removed their shoes as a symbol of their sorrow. By placing shoes on his son's feet, the father was making an announcement to his son: "The time of mourning and the days of separation are over! The time of rejoicing has come!"

In this action we see the teaching of God's heart toward us: *God rejoices over us!* He rejoices at our return and at the restored relationship we share with Him (see Zeph. 3:17).

Through the story of the prodigal son, Jesus illustrates our standing before God: We are welcomed to a place of confidence through the forgiveness given to us through Christ. Our Father offers us an authoritative right to be sons (John 1:12), to function in partnership with Him and to extend His dominion over all the earth. No matter what we fight, whether the powers of hell or our own weaknesses, eventual victory will be ours.

This is what Jesus wants to teach us when He instructs us to pray "Our Father in heaven." He is founding all prayer on a growing relationship with a loving God. And as the truth of God's reception and our restoration fills us, we will discover yet another benefit: We will learn to receive each other. We begin, with Christ's help, to see one another as brothers and sisters who have been received by a loving Father. And in that light, we cannot help but join together in harmony, lifting up a concert of powerful, effective prayer as people who have discovered God's love and who are learning to pray confidently in Him.

TRANSFORMING FAITH

Be holy in all your conduct, because it is written,
"Be holy, for I am holy."

1 PETER 1:15,16

HALLOWED BE YOUR NAME

The frequently intoned phrase "hallowed be Your name" literally means "Holy be Your name." In these words we are invited to experience the transforming power of prayer, as Jesus introduces us to life's mightiest action: worship. "Holy be Your name" is a call to worship at the throne of God.

It will better help us to understand worship when we realize that the throne of God is an actual place. We are not offering our worship to some mysterious place "up there somewhere." In Revelation 4:8, John describes his glorious vision of God's throne and the mighty angelic beings around it. An innumerable host is seen worshiping God, saying:

Holy, holy, holy,
Lord God Almighty,
Who was and is and is to come!

It is to this place that Jesus invites us, not in an imaginary sense, but in a living, dynamic sense of worship. We are called to gather before our Father and to bring Him our own offerings of praise.

Psalm 22:3 (*NASB*) helps explain why worship is so important and so potentially transforming of our life and circumstance. The text teaches that through their worship, God's people may literally make an earthly place for Him to be enthroned in the midst of them:

> Yet Thou art holy, O Thou who art enthroned upon the praises of Israel.

Here we see that the dynamic objective of worship isn't simply an exercise in religious forms; instead, worship is God's assigned way to bring His presence and power to His people. In other words, just as we enter into God's presence with worship, so He responds by coming into our presence. Our worship invites Him to rule in our midst. When our hearts are opened wide in worship, God will respond. His presence and power will come to transform—to change us and our circumstances.

So we see a dual objective for worship: (1) to declare God's *transcendent* greatness and (2) to receive His *transforming* power in our lives, situations and needs.

In a dynamic sense, the words "Holy be Your name" are both an exalting of God and a humbling of ourselves. When we use those words, we are inviting the Holy Spirit to make God's presence and Person real in our midst. Such encounters on a regular basis can only bring transformation—the conforming of our wills to God's and the shaping of our lives into His likeness:

> But we all, with unveiled face, beholding as in a mirror the glory of the Lord, are being transformed into the same image from glory to glory, just as by the Spirit of the Lord (2 Cor. 3:18).

Worship by itself cannot bring about this transformation we need in order to respond to the Word, obey the Holy Spirit and walk in obedience daily; but worship *can* bring it about faster.

To better understand transformation through worshiping, let's first examine the meaning of holiness, since that is the trait of God's nature that Jesus focuses on in this section of the Lord's Prayer.

As often as "holy" is used as a worship expression, it is too seldom understood. We tend to think of holiness as an external characteristic, such as a meditative expression, an organlike tone of speech or a certain style of garment. This restrictive view causes many of us to feel intimidated or disqualified, because we feel we haven't the necessary external traits of holiness to earn God's pleasure.

Others consider holiness to be a stern, forbidding trait of God's nature, a sort of attitudinal barrier on God's part—an obstacle created by His flaunting His perfection in the face of our weaknesses and sins. This, too, is incorrect.

Simply stated, holiness is shown in the Bible as relating to God's *completeness*. That is, God's holiness essentially acknowledges

It is clear that he does not pray, who, far from uplifting himself to God, requires that God shall lower Himself to him, and who resorts to prayer not to stir the man in us to will what God wills, but only to persuade God to will what the man in us wills.

ST. THOMAS AQUINAS
1225(?)-1274

that He is complete; there is nothing lacking in His person, and nothing needs to be added to make Him "enough." This meaning of holiness holds a promise: *Because* God's holiness is complete and because it is His nature to give, He wants to share His holiness with us to complete *us!* His holiness, then, is not an obstacle to our acceptance but rather a resource for our completion and fulfillment as persons. God is ready to pour Himself into us, to complete those areas of our lives that are lacking, or unholy, because of our sin.

As we open ourselves through worship to this desired work of God, we will find His holiness and wholeness overtaking our unholiness. His personal power, in response to our worship, will begin to sweep away whatever residue remains from the destruction caused by our sinful past.

As we approach Him in worship-filled prayer, a spiritual genesis begins to take effect. The traits and characteristics born in us when we became part of God's family will begin to grow, making us more and more like Him. Just as surely as physical traits are transmitted to us by our earthly parents, so the nature and likeness of our heavenly Father will grow in us as we learn and grow in our worship of Him.

This truth is reflected in the command "Be holy, for I am holy" (Lev. 11:45; 1 Pet. 1:16), which holds a promise of holiness and completeness. This edict is not so much a demand that we stretch ourselves through self-produced devices of holiness as it is God's guarantee that His life in us will become increasingly evident and powerfully transforming.

So in teaching us the Lord's Prayer, Jesus calls us into the Father's presence to give the Father the opportunity to remake us in His likeness.

That's transformation—a transformation that allows God to extend His kingdom through us. And this personal dimension of transformation is only the beginning.

Beyond the power of worship-filled prayer to change *us,* it can also achieve a remarkable impact on *others.* In instructing us to enter the Father's presence with worship, Jesus points the way to a faith that can transform all of our lives and the lives of those whom we encounter. He says, "Since God is your Father, let your worship in His presence make you more like Him; and as you do, His working in you will affect those around you."

Let us enter His presence with worship! Let's take the faith-filled step that moves us to experience the transforming power of God's rule in our lives and character through our faithful prayers.

So take a new stance. Move your posture in worship beyond one of passive reflection to one of power-filled potential for *transformation.* The holy One we hallow in prayer is ready to invade every situation we address with His *completing* presence and power.

RESPONSIBLE FAITH

Therefore, since we are receiving a kingdom which cannot be shaken,
let us have grace, by which we may serve God acceptably
with reverence and godly fear.

HEBREWS 12:28

YOUR KINGDOM COME, YOUR WILL BE DONE ON EARTH AS IT IS IN HEAVEN

The Lord's Prayer shows us how Christ intends us to effectively discharge our responsibility in prayer. "Your kingdom come. Your will be done on earth as it is in heaven" (Matt. 6:10). Jesus' counsel on how to pray illuminates a truth that we often ignore: People need to invite God's rule and power into the affairs of their lives through prayer. For if humans won't pray, God's rule in their circumstances is forfeited.

That thought runs counter to the common supposition, *Well, if God wants to do something, He'll just do it.* This sorry strain of fatalism infests most minds. But the idea of man as a pawn moved by the Almighty at His whim is *totally* removed from the truth revealed in Scripture.

Jesus shows us that every human being is responsible for inviting God's rule—i.e., His benevolent purpose, presence and power—into this world. Rather than portraying men and women as hopeless, helpless victims of circumstance, the Bible declares that redeemed persons are hopeful and capable of expecting victory when they pray in faith. The grounds for this understanding can be found at the beginning of the Bible. There we find why Jesus teaches us to pray for the reinstatement of God's role on Earth as in heaven.

Man's Loss

In Genesis 1, the Bible tells us that dominion over this planet was given to man by God Himself (see Gen. 1:28). This assignment was not only one of great privilege but also one that essentially made mankind responsible for what would happen on Earth. Unless we understand this fact, we will never really understand that most of the confusion, agony and distress in our world today exists as a direct result of our having betrayed God's initial entrusting of Earth to us. As a race, we have violated the responsibility God gave us.

This betrayal began at the fall of man. Through that tragedy we have suffered inestimable loss. Man not only lost his relationship with God, but he also lost his ability to rule responsibly. Man's ability and authority to successfully administrate God's rule over the earth is completely frustrated—whether the issue is environmental pollution or home and family management. And this lost capacity for a peaceful, healthful life has an added complication.

According to the Bible, "the whole world lies under the sway of the wicked one" (1 John 5:19). We not only betrayed our God-given trust of ruling the earth, we also lost to the devil the administration intended for us as humankind (under God's rule). Since the Fall, mankind has not only been vulnerable to satanic deceptions, but by our own sin and rebellion we have also contributed to the confused mess our world has become. Between man's sinning and Satan's hateful quest to obliterate, death and destruction have invaded every part of life as we know it—breaking relationships, dashing hopes and dreams and ruining destinies.

God's Restoration

But when man's betrayal of God's trust turned this world over to the powers of death and hell, God lovingly provided us with hope: a living option in the person of His Son. God sent Jesus, whose ministry announced the possibility of man's restoration to God's kingdom:

> Repent, for the kingdom of heaven is at hand (Matt. 4:17).

In that statement, Jesus made it clear that the rule of God was once again being made available to mankind. No longer did any member of the race need to remain a hopeless victim of sin and hell!

In His ministry, both then and now, Jesus manifests every aspect of the kingdom He offers. When Jesus heals, He shows what can happen when the rule of God enters a situation. When He answers need in any dimension, He is putting into action the power of God's rule available to our lives. As Jesus teaches, His

He that seeks God in everything is sure to find God in everything. When we thus live wholly unto God, God is wholly ours and we are then happy in all the happiness of God; for by uniting with Him in heart, and will, and spirit, we are united to all that He is and has in Himself. This is the purity and perfection of life that we pray for in the Lord's Prayer, that God's kingdom may come and His will be done in us, as it is in Heaven. And this we may be sure is not only necessary, but attainable by us, or our Saviour would not have made it a part of our daily prayer.

WILLIAM LAW
1686-1761

objective is always to help straighten out our thinking ("repent"), to help us see what Father God is really like so that we might respond correctly to Him and His kingdom.

But at the same time that Jesus ministers, hell seeks to level its hostile devices against the Messiah and the kingdom He offers. Consequently, Jesus demonstrates a warlike opposition to the invisible powers of darkness. He is well known for demonstrating God's love, but He is equally well known for the way He confronts the demonic powers of hell. Colossians 2:15 says that in the climactic act of His crucifixion, Christ smashed these powers, making possible the offer of reentry into divine life with God and paving the way for us, His followers, to also strike down the satanic powers we encounter (see Mark 16:17-20).

Man's Responsibility

In light of these truths, each person must decide whether or not he or she will draw on the resources of Christ's triumph through the Cross and live to advance God's kingdom in this world. Acceptance of Christ *begins* our participation in His kingdom (John 3:3-5); we are then called to *advance* it, as we share the gospel of Christ with the world around us (see Matt. 28:19; Acts 1:8). There is no more effective way to accelerate this advance than for believers to pray together!

Our first steps in faith are made on the feet of prayer, whether we are moving into victory or into witness. Our ongoing growth in prayer comes with recognizing that faith and victory are *not* achieved merely through the zeal of human programs but, instead, by prayer that acknowledges the triumph of Calvary as a release for God's presence and power.

This is why Jesus instructs us to pray "Your kingdom come." With this prayer we are taking on our role as members of a race that once betrayed the King and forfeited His intended purposes to the adversary. But now He has endowed us, His redeemed sons and daughters, with restored Kingdom authority through prayer to welcome His entry into every need and pain of this planet.

The power is God's, but the privilege and responsibility to pray are ours. So let us hear and understand Jesus' words and come together at His throne, expecting and receiving the flow of the Holy Spirit's power! By His anointing we will find enablement to see God's purposes being accomplished through us and our prayers.

This is what it means to pray "Thy kingdom come": to see the rule and power of the kingdom of God as present and practical, to see the personal possibilities for prayer in every dimension of our daily lives. Let us never allow the promise of Christ's future kingdom to keep us from possessing the dimensions of victory that God has for us *now*. Jesus is coming again to establish His kingdom over all the earth! But that should not cause us to neglect our present prayer or ministry responsibilities for advancing the gospel.

Until He comes again, Jesus directed us to "occupy" (Luke 19:13, *KJV*). Our role as an occupation force entails drawing on the resources of God's kingdom and power, reaching into the realm of the invisible through prayer and changing one circumstance after another.

"Your kingdom come. Your will be done on earth as it is in heaven." It is our privilege to pray this and our responsibility thereby to exercise the beginning of our reinstatement to partnership with God—to see the tangled affairs of this planet reversed from the fallen order to God's intended order.

DEPENDENT FAITH

It is written, "Man shall not live by bread alone, but by every word that proceeds from the mouth of God."

MATTHEW 4:4

GIVE US THIS DAY OUR DAILY BREAD

In these words, Jesus is talking about more than our having enough food or having our physical needs met. He is issuing an invitation for us, as children of God, to come to the Father daily for refreshing, renewal and nourishment for both our souls and our bodies. This phrase, "Give us this day our daily bread" (Matt. 6:11), registers a specific command for us to recognize our dependency on the Lord for *all* nourishment and to realize that this provision for our needs flows out of the discipline of daily prayer.

James 4:2 makes a strong statement regarding the necessity of prayer: "You do not have because you do not ask." The Lord is ready to release many things to us, but His readiness doesn't remove our place or need of asking. In other words, the promise of God's care for us does not bypass our need for prayerful, acknowledged dependence. The Lord Jesus teaches us to turn willingly to the Father and call out in prayer for Him to work in our lives. Rather than relying on our own strength (chin up, teeth clenched, saying, "I'm going to get this done"), we need to come to the Father in prayer—daily, dependently and gratefully.

Dependent prayer is not desperate or demeaning prayer. It is neither frantic (as though we only turned to God in a crisis, as a last resort) nor depersonalizing (as though God required us to grovel in

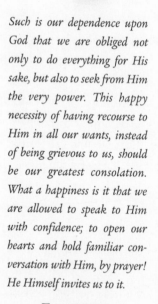

Such is our dependence upon God that we are obliged not only to do everything for His sake, but also to seek from Him the very power. This happy necessity of having recourse to Him in all our wants, instead of being grievous to us, should be our greatest consolation. What a happiness is it that we are allowed to speak to Him with confidence; to open our hearts and hold familiar conversation with Him, by prayer! He Himself invites us to it.

FRANCOIS
FENELON
1651-1715

order to escape His wrath). In contrast to these distorted views, dependent prayer is the *way* we gain a personal realization of God's unswerving commitment to us and *how* we participate in God's promised provision for us.

Psalm 90:12 says, "Teach us to number our days, that we may gain a heart of wisdom." This is a sound-minded request for wisdom to recognize how *few* days we have and how much we need to employ them wisely. In the Lord's Prayer, the words "Give us this day" show our need to learn an accountability for each day's hours and events, as surely as our need for having adequacy of food and other needs. Dependent prayer can help us do this. Jesus is not merely teaching us to request "bread" morning, noon and night. He is teaching us to ask for the Father's direction and provision in every event and during each hour of our day.

Committing each day's details to God in prayer—requesting today's bread—can deliver us from pointless pursuits and wasted time. Such prayer paves the way to victorious days.

> My times are in Your hand; deliver me from the hand of
> my enemies (Ps. 31:15).

What wisdom! When we put our day in God's hands, any enemy we face can be conquered. Whether the enemy is ourselves—procrastination, sloth or other weaknesses—or the enemy is a demonic conspiracy Satan has plotted against us, *our Lord is able to deliver us!*

"Daily bread" prayer is "daily victory" and "daily overcoming" prayer, because we are drawing on God's full provision for our sufficiency. He will help us to overcome anything that might wrench our lives from His purpose or cause valuable time to slip through our fingers.

Submit your day to the Lord and ask Him to provide for your needs. Whether your need is food or counsel for the day's activities, you will find that it *will* be provided. He will faithfully and abundantly respond as we set our times in His hands.

And when you learn to pray this way, you will find another wonderful promise being fulfilled:

> As your days, so shall your strength be (Deut. 33:25).

Learning to pray "Give us this day our daily bread" finds in the Lord a strength proportionate to each day's needs. Whatever challenges a day holds—confrontations, difficulties, even tragedies—we will receive the strength to face them. Just as we derive physical strength and nourishment from eating daily bread, so we will gain spiritual strength and nourishment when we learn the wisdom of acknowledging our dependency upon the Father—and pray His way.

RELEASING FAITH

Their sins and their lawless deeds I will remember no more.

HEBREWS 10:17

AND FORGIVE US OUR DEBTS, AS WE FORGIVE OUR DEBTORS

The next point in the Lord's Prayer addresses our need for forgiveness. Some people use the word "trespasses," while most translations use the word "debts" for this section of the prayer (Matt. 6:12). Both expressions are accurate and significant. In fact, we need to pray both ways, for in these two expressions we see the two sides of human disobedience: sins of *commission* and sins of *omission*—wrong things we have done and right things we have neglected to do.

"Forgive us our trespasses" speaks to our need of asking the Lord to forgive us for our having "stepped over the line." God is concerned about trespassing because He wants to keep us from the things that will damage or destroy us. In His Word He sets clear, protective guidelines—territorial boundaries, if you will—that say, "Do not trespass here." When we violate these commands intended to help us avoid that which is self-destructive, we are guilty of sins of commission.

On the other hand, "forgive us our debts" relates to our failures, to cases where it might be said that we owed it to the situation to do better than we did. But in failing to act rightly, we have become debtors. And such indebtedness can hang like a cloud over the soul, hindering our sense of freedom and faith for the future.

With this phrase of asking forgiveness, Christ fashions this dual dimension of release into our regular pattern of prayer: a request for release from both the shame of guilt and the pain of neglect.

But in order to grasp the power potential in this prayer for forgiveness, we need to see that both of the phrases—"forgive us our debts" and "as we forgive our debtors"—are conditionally linked.

Jesus specifically teaches that the degree of our forgiveness— our willingness to release others—establishes a standard of measurement. He gives back to us that measure of release and forgiveness that we show to others. And this fact brings us to the heart of life's most practical truth: *If I do not move in God's dimension of release and forgiveness toward others, I will inevitably become an obstruction to my own life, growth and fruitfulness.*

See it, dear one. Forgiving faith goes both ways: We must confess our own violations against God, and we must forgive others whom we believe have violated us.

FORGIVENESS AND GRACE

Notice that by emphasizing our need for forgiveness of sin, Jesus isn't shaking a stick of condemnation in our faces. The fact of our guilt isn't the issue. The real problem is that we need to be taught to pray for forgiveness.

We are all people bent from God's original design and purpose. Not one of us is flawless; no one is without selfishness and pride. Sin is an inherited inclination in us all, and it needs to be forgiven. The call to pray this prayer is the promise that it will be answered. We need to pray, "Forgive me, Father," and we need to pray it often. However, the Lord's Prayer is not meant to level a focus on guilt but rather on grace.

Jesus taught us to pray for forgiveness on a regular basis, not to remind us of our sinfulness, but to keep us from becoming sloppy in our ideas about the grace of God. We often distort God's grace and give in to the deception that we can do anything we want as long as God's grace encompasses us. But in Romans 6:1,2, the apostle Paul demands pointedly, "What shall we say then? Shall we continue in sin that grace may abound? Certainly not! How shall we who died to sin live any longer in it?"

In calling us to pray "Forgive us our trespasses," Jesus isn't seeking to remind us of our failures; but He *does* want to sensitize us to sin and to the fact that sin hinders our growth in Him.

God's forgiveness is graciously offered and abundantly available. In the Scriptures He warmly invites us to pardon, cleansing and release:

> As far as the east is from the west, so far has He removed our transgressions from us (Ps. 103:12).

> He will again have compassion on us, and will subdue our iniquities (Mic. 7:19).

> If we confess our sins, He is faithful and just to forgive us our sins and to cleanse us from all unrighteousness (1 John 1:9).

Forgiveness can be counted on. The condition—*confession*—is presented clearly, and the availability is promised: He can be depended on to forgive us.

FORGIVENESS AND RECONCILIATION

Jesus also describes forgiveness as being relayed *through* us to others. God's Word expands and applies the truth that we who have received forgiveness need to be forgiving.

Jesus directs us to go to anyone who has something against us and, in an attitude of humility and forgiveness, rectify our relationship with that person. And He says this must be done before we can make any serious, honest approach to Him in worship:

> Therefore if you bring your gift to the altar, and there remember that your brother has something against you, leave your gift there before the altar, and go your way. First be reconciled to your brother, and then come and offer your gift (Matt. 5:23,24).

> And whenever you stand praying, if you have anything against anyone, forgive him, that your Father in heaven may also forgive you your trespasses (Mark 11:25).

When we go to another for reconciliation, we must be certain we are not doing so in an attempt to justify ourselves. If someone has a difference of opinion or other problem with us, regardless of whose fault it is, God will not allow us to make any charge against that person. Christ desires that we be willing to go the extra mile and assume the role of reconciler—just as He did for us in reconciling us to the Father.

Understand that people often perceive a situation as the opposite of how it really is; this will help you to act as Christ commands. For example, if you have been offended, you may be completely unaware of the viewpoint of the person who has hurt you. To the other person, it will often seem as though *he* or *she* was the one violated and that *you* are at fault.

The effects of sin and Satan's discord in our lives makes us all terribly vulnerable to natural misunderstandings, and we need to learn this point of human understanding. We must acknowledge it in order to open up the reconciling process. Then, when we become willing to go to others (recognizing that their attitudes toward us are likely based on something they perceive as being *our* fault), when we accept the burden of the misunderstanding (as Jesus did to bring peace between God and man), *a real release will be realized.*

Let's learn to accept the responsibility for whatever dispute has breached our relationships with others. Restored relationships are possible when in Christlike manner, we live out the meaning in this lesson: *Forgive me as I forgive others.*

Naturally, there may be times when the most loving, scriptural stand we can take is to confront others with their wrongdoing. Jesus did so, and the Holy Spirit will show us when we are to do so. But the spirit of forgiveness never does this in a self-defensive way; rather, it operates in a spirit of reconciliation.

This Kingdom order of forgiveness will not always be easy.

By nature we all prefer to be in the driver's seat, so to speak, and the ministry of reconciliation always puts us at the mercy of the *other person's* responses instead.

It has been well said that no man ever sank under the burden of the day. It is when tomorrow's burden is added to the burden of today that the weight is more than a man can bear. Never load yourselves so, my friends. If you find yourselves so loaded, at least remember this: it is your own doing, not God's. He begs you to leave the future to Him and mind the present.

GEORGE
MACDONALD
SCOTTISH NOVELIST AND POET
1824-1905

But this is exactly where Jesus put Himself when He laid down His life to make forgiveness available to us. Though God hasn't called us to be someone's doormat, we *are* called to learn Christ's pathway to dominion. To do so is to see that this Kingdom path to power is in the spirit of the Lamb, never in one of self-defense.

There is no greater step upward in faith than the one we take when we learn to forgive—and *do it*. Forgiveness blesses people who need our love and acceptance, and it releases us to bright horizons of joy, health and dynamic faith in prayer.

OBEDIENT FAITH

The Lord knows how to deliver the godly out of temptations and to reserve the unjust under punishment for the day of judgment.

2 PETER 2:9

AND DO NOT LEAD US INTO TEMPTATION, BUT DELIVER US FROM THE EVIL ONE

Our next step brings us to the most paradoxical part of the Lord's Prayer: "And do not lead us into temptation, but deliver us from the evil one" (Matt. 6:13). At first these words seem a bit confusing in light of other Scriptures that assure us God does not tempt anyone. James 1:13,14 makes this clear: God tempts no man, but when we are tempted, we are drawn away of our own lusts and enticed.

We know, then, that in teaching us to pray, "Lead us not into temptation," Jesus is not teaching us that we must beg God not to trick us into sinning. Nor is Jesus teaching us a prayer for escaping the demands of growth that come through God's leading us—and He *does* lead us—into trials.

To understand what Jesus *is* teaching we must first gain a clear understanding of the word "temptation," a word that carries a two-sided meaning. First, temptation essentially has to do with the desire of an adversary to test and break through our defenses. Second, temptation deals with the strength gained through encountering an adversary; that is, when the one who is tested overcomes the test, the resulting victory builds strength. Temptation, therefore, is both positive and negative, depending on our viewpoint and response.

In that light, Jesus isn't suggesting that we should ask or expect to avoid the kind of confrontation He faced with Satan. In fact, the Bible tells us that the Holy Spirit *led* Christ into that experience of conflict with the devil (see Matt. 4:1). As a direct result of overcoming this time of temptation, Jesus was brought to a place of victory and dominion over the enemy (see John 14:30). So, clearly, this section of the Lord's Prayer holds a promise of victory, rather than a plea for relief from struggle.

We are not asking God, "Please don't play with us as pawns on a chess board, risking our loss by leading us into questionable situations." Instead, if we examine various translations of this challenging verse and note the tense and mood of the Greek verb translated "lead" or "bring unto," we will discover that the phrase "lead us not into temptation" is a guarantee of victory— if we'll take it!

A clear translation of these words shows that Jesus is actually directing us to pray, "Father, should we at any point be led into temptation, test or trial, we want to come out delivered and victorious."

So the issue in this portion of the Lord's Prayer is a questioning not of God's character but, rather, *ours*. Such a prayer is saying, "Lord, You won't lead or introduce me into any situations but those for my refinement, growth and victory. Therefore, when I encounter circumstances designed to lead me astray, I will recognize that it is not Your will for me to walk that way. God, I am committing myself in advance to *want* victory, to *seek* deliverance and to *take* the way of escape You have promised me":

No temptation has overtaken you except such as is common to man; but God is faithful, who will not allow you to be tempted beyond what you are able, but with the temptation will also make the way of escape, that you may be able to bear it (1 Cor. 10:13).

Here, then, is obedient faith confronting the reality of our vulnerability to temptation. It's sometimes so quick in its rise and so subtle in its approach that Jesus' prayer lesson teaches us our need to have our steps established in advance through regular prayer. With these words, "lead us not," we come to the Lord in advance and commit ourselves to receive His deliverances rather than allow temptation to entangle us in its snares. This prayer doesn't question God's nature or leading but, instead, declares we are casting ourselves on Him.

It's important to understand the intent of this prayer because man is so easily deluded

We will do better in dealing with temptations if we keep an eye on them in the very beginning. Temptations are more easily overcome if they are never allowed to enter our minds. Meet them at the door as soon as they knock, and do not let them in.

THOMAS À KEMPIS
1380-1471

by temptation. Once again, Jesus isn't suggesting it is God's nature to trick or corrupt us by tempting us. In fact, He is emphasizing it is God's nature to "deliver us from evil." The prayer simply establishes a commitment on our part to receive the triumphant life Christ offers us in dominion over evil. Our lives become more effective when we avoid being neutralized by hell's manipulations or by our flesh's cry for self-indulgence.

This prayer doesn't remove temptation's challenge, but it does help us understand that we aren't evil simply because we're tempted. Furthermore, we have a certain promise: God has a doorway of exit for us. When temptation comes, the prayer "deliver us from evil" ensures us a way out.

What a great certainty this is! What a beautiful climax to this lesson in the Lord's Prayer!

> And the Lord will deliver me from every evil work and preserve me for His heavenly kingdom. To Him be glory forever and ever. Amen! (2 Tim. 4:18).

If we seek Him, God *will* deliver us out of temptation! Thus, when we pray "deliver us from evil," we are committing ourselves to walk in triumph and dominion over the things that would seek to conquer us—to live in obedient faith. And to live this way is to count on God's deliverance, for He is able (see Heb 2:18)!

TRUSTING FAITH

Therefore humble yourselves under the mighty hand of God,
that He may exalt you in due time.

1 PETER 5:6

FOR YOURS IS THE KINGDOM AND THE POWER AND THE GLORY FOREVER

Our study of the Lord's Prayer concludes with these words of trusting faith: "For Yours is the kingdom and the power and the glory forever" (Matt. 6:13). Here is the active expression of a heart that has absolute assurance of the complete triumph of God—in *His* time.

Turn with me to Acts 1:6,7. I think the words of Jesus to His disciples will give us additional insight into this section of the Lord's Prayer:

Therefore, when they had come together, they asked Him, saying, "Lord, will You at this time restore the kingdom to Israel?" And He said to them, "It is not for you to know times or seasons which the Father has put in His own authority."

Jesus spoke these words following His resurrection, as He was giving final instructions to His disciples before His ascension. He had been explaining principles of the kingdom of God, and the disciples had gotten confused (see Acts 1:3-5). In light of what He was teaching and with the facts of the Crucifixion and the Resurrection behind them, Jesus' disciples inquired: "Just when will this kingdom finally come?" They probably felt sure that the time *must* be ripe for the messianic kingdom to be established. Surely now was the time for Israel to be liberated from Roman oppression!

But Jesus patiently replied that it wasn't for them to know when His kingdom would be established (v. 7). He wasn't stalling them. Nor was He denying the ultimate establishment of His kingdom someday. But He was redirecting their understanding.

The issue of the Kingdom's coming with power is asserted in His very next words:

> But you shall receive power when the Holy Spirit has come upon you; and you shall be witnesses to Me in Jerusalem, and in all Judea and Samaria, and to the end of the earth (Acts 1:8).

He was showing them the Holy Spirit's coming was a mission to work the *spread* of the kingdom *through* them, not the *completion* of the kingdom *for* them.

This conversation between Jesus and His disciples, with Jesus' promise of the Holy Spirit's power in relation to the timing of His kingdom, can help us understand the meaning of the concluding phrase of the Lord's Prayer. We can see that Jesus was teaching the pathway to trust—to the knowledge that when we have prayed in faith, we can rest firm in our confidence God has heard. He *will* attend to all issues; and even when we don't see *our* timing in the answer, *His* purposes aren't being lost.

Consider the words "Yours is the kingdom."

For many, these words seem to point to the future. But Jesus taught very clearly that in certain respects the presence and power of His kingdom are given to us *now*: "Do not fear, little flock, for it is your Father's good pleasure to give you the kingdom" (Luke 12:32). Although we will only experience the fullest expression of His kingdom when He comes again, we mustn't diminish the fact that this prayer is dealing with God's rule and power impacting situations *now*. Wherever the Spirit is given room and allowed to work, the Kingdom "comes."

So here, at prayer, Jesus is reminding us that such privileged participation in the power of His kingdom life has terms: We are called to submit to God's rule in our lives (see 1 Pet. 5:6).

THE POWER AND THE GLORY

The first factor in developing a trusting faith is learning that the rule, the power and the glory are God's. He allows us to share with Him, but He is Lord. He gives us power, but only He is omnipotent. He teaches us, but He alone is all-knowing. And submission and humility are prerequisites to sharing God's authority. Satan flees the believer who has learned the truth of "Yours is the power" (see Jas. 4:7).

Faith is ever and always challenging the status quo where evil reigns, where pain and sickness prevail, where hatred and hellishness rule or where human failure breeds confusion. As we learn to live under the Holy Spirit's rule, we will be able to take a bold, confrontive stance against all in opposition to that rule whether demon, flesh or earthly circumstance. Such a stance says, "I rely upon the One who claims ultimate and final rule everywhere. I won't give way to any lie that attempts to cast doubt on God's ultimate, complete victory." And when we do this, we will often see results that would not have been realized without Kingdom praying.

Even if all the things that people prayed for happened—which they do not—this would not prove what Christians mean by the efficacy of prayer. For prayer is request. The essence of request, as distinct from compulsion, is that it may or may not be granted. And if an infinitely wise Being listens to the requests of finite and foolish creatures, of course He will sometimes grant and sometimes refuse them. Invariable "success" in prayer would not prove the Christian doctrine at all. It would prove something more like magic—a power in certain human beings to control, or compel, the course of nature.

C. S. LEWIS
1898-1963

But what about when we don't see any results? What then? The disciples' inquiry echoes from our lips, too: "Will the Kingdom be now?"

In answer to this question, Jesus teaches us to pray, "Yours is the kingdom." He's leading us to realize that even though answers may not yet fully appear, two things come from trusting faith: (1) the knowledge that the ultimate triumph of God's manifest power shall come in His time and (2) the assurance that until that time, He has given us His Spirit to enable us to do His will.

Here is our fortress of confidence. Though time may pass without our seeing "victory" as we would interpret it, we know—and pray with praise—that we have not been deserted! God's Holy Spirit brings us His presence and power right now, for whatever circumstances we encounter.

There will be times when we will see God's kingdom power in action—with healings and miracles—in our lives. But there will also be times the Lord simply says, "Trust Me—the time is not yet, but in the meantime the power of My Spirit will sustain you."

Great power and privilege are given to the Church. "Nothing will be impossible for you," Jesus says (Matt. 17:20). Yet, as certain as the promise and possibilities are, we must humbly and honestly acknowledge there are times when we seem unable to *possess* the promise. Such acknowledgments are not statements of doubt. Nor are they cases of God's refusing to grant us an answer or fulfill His Word.

God's promises are true and His Word is faithful! But the Kingdom timing is His, too! And so are the ultimate power and glory.

When we conclude the Lord's Prayer with "Yours is the kingdom and the power and the glory," we aren't being either passive or merely poetic. We are reflecting the power of trusting faith—faith that stands in firm confidence, regardless of circumstances. Such faith declares, "Lord, to You belongs all Kingdom authority, for You are the possessor of all! And as I gain that Kingdom, a portion at a time, I trust You—for the Kingdom is Yours."

There are no greater grounds for rest and contentment in life than the certainty wrapped in these words:

"Yours is the kingdom"—all rule *belongs* to God.

"Yours is the power"—all mightiness *flows* from Him.

"Yours is the glory"—His victory *shall be* complete.

With this kind of prayer comes boldness, confidence and rest. For when all is said and done, our greatest resource is to rest in God's greatness. In Him we find confidence that our every need will be met, our ultimate victory realized and—in His time, by His purpose and for His glory—all things will resolve unto His wisest, richest and best.

So let us now and ever join the angelic throng around His throne, uniting our concert of prayer and praise with theirs (see Rev. 4:8), saying:

Holy, holy, holy!
Who was,
Who is,
Who is to come—
The Almighty!

JESUS' LESSONS ON BOLD FAITH

Let us therefore come boldly to the throne of grace, that we may obtain
mercy and find grace to help in time of need.

HEBREWS 4:16

As is my usual habit, I awoke early for the purpose of prayer. But when I sat on the edge of the bed, I heard a whisper to my heart: *You have forgotten the discipline of daily devotional habit.*

I knew immediately what the Holy Spirit was dealing with me about. And though the prompting to some might have seemed a rebuke, I didn't protest. Because I understood He was speaking to me about my personal walk with Jesus. The issue was being *quiet* and *with* Him as compared to passionately praying about issues and asking for answers. There is a difference.

DAILY DEVOTIONAL HABIT

It was as though God was saying, "I am not just looking, Jack, for your petitions and powerful, passionate prayer. I will honor your seeking to see My kingdom enter the world, as you pray for the invasion of My power into hell's darkness. And I do welcome your worship as you extol My name. But Child, I wish you would simply spend more time with *Me*—to know My heart and let Me deal with yours, to give you instructions in the personal matters of your private life as you learn to *wait* on Me."

Now, I had not been totally closed off to simply being in the Lord's presence. But I had become so excited, indeed zealous, in the application of great principles of supplication, intercession and faith's confession (things I'd begun to learn and practice) that the *power* potential in prayer was distracting me from the *devotional* aspect of a personal walk with Jesus. But now, the Lord was reminding me of His desire for *me:* "I just want you to be with Me."

Daybreak is a booklet I wrote following that encounter, a handbook outlining details for a daily devotional habit. It points to a more personal and intimate walk with the Lord—one in which we bring our days to Him, to allow Him to order our steps, as we learn to function in the wisdom of daily devotions in the presence of Jesus. All prayer is best cultivated on the foundation of a quiet time. During regular quiet times with the Savior, relationship becomes deepened and established in a personal dimension.

By reason of that small book's abundant availability and inexpensive price, I will not elaborate the patterns for my daily devotional habit here. However, the following outline from the book provides a simple structure to prompt your private, personal walk with Jesus—your "talk time" with the Savior:

I. Enter His Presence

Begin by presenting yourself with thanksgiving and praise, placing your whole being before God (see Mark 12:30).

A. Find a new reason every day to do this (see Pss. 100:4; 118:24).

B. Present your body in worship to Him (see Ps. 63:3,4; Rom. 12:1).

       C. Sing a new song to the Lord (see Ps. 96:1,2; Col. 3:16).

       D. Allow the Holy Spirit to assist your praise (see 1 Cor. 14:15; Jude 20).

II. Open Your Heart

Present your heart to God with confession for cleansing, and diligently seek purity (see Prov. 4:23).

       A. Invite the Lord to search your heart (see Ps. 139:23,24).

       B. Recognize the danger of deception (see Jer. 17:9; 1 John 1:6-10).

       C. Set a monitor on your mouth and heart (see Pss. 19:14; 49:3).

       D. Keep Christ's purposes and goal in view (see Ps. 90:12; Phil. 3:13,14).

III. Order Your Day

In obedience to our Lord, present your day and submit to His ways and rule in your life (see 1 Pet. 5:6-11).

       A. Surrender your day to God (see Deut. 33:25; Pss. 31:14,15; 37:4,5).

       B. Indicate your dependence on Him (see Ps. 131:1-3; Prov. 3:5-7).

       C. Request specific direction for today (see Ps. 25:4,5; Isa. 30:21).

       D. Obey Jesus' explicit instructions (see Matt. 6:11; 7:7,8).

Taking these simple pointers, allow yourself regular times to be "up and early with the Lord." Never let the adversary condemn you because you miss one or more days. Let every time you *are* with the Savior be as precious to you as He wants it to be.

You will find that early morning hours are usually best to find unbroken, undisturbed occasions for quiet in His presence. It was Jesus' pattern, and it deserves emulation (see Mark 1:35). And remember, use the above outline for a guideline, not a regimented requirement. I've found it helps to target Him (His presence), my heart (and purity) and my days (His counsel about the details of my life).

In the environment of this kind of walk with Christ, boldness of faith and expanding intercessory prayer will grow. Petitionary requests—however simple or complex—will become confident requests when we simply come to know Jesus. So with this resource in hand and intimacy as our priority, the beginning of a prayer discipline is in place.

PERSEVERANCE IN PRAYER

Moving forward from this foundation, a disciple's growth in prayer will broaden in its dimensions. Ephesians 6:18 tells us to be "praying always with all prayer and supplication in the Spirit, being watchful to this end with all perseverance and supplication." Because of the importance of the idea presented here and because of the false images surrounding a key word to understanding this passage, let's study the matter of perseverance.

In this text, the word means steadfastness, constancy and continuing much time in prayer. The idea is clear and should be readily understood. But the concept of perseverance is still often twisted in some people's thinking to mean something other than keeping at it.

Some mistakenly view persevering in prayer as a gutsy, grit-your-teeth, "I'll hang tough till God finally hears me and does something" kind of exercise. Misunderstanding perseverance and persistence can also breed a sense that it is a complaint about our state of affairs: "God, I've been praying for a long time. Can't You see where things are? I need help, I need it now, and I am tired of waiting!" One view supposes *earning* an answer; the other supposes we can or ought to "bully" God. But heaven really doesn't need this exhortation from us. God is never passive.

Yet the idea has somehow evolved that perseverance in prayer is needed in order either to gain God's approval or somehow to win His interest. Curiously, two of Jesus' parables have been used to support this distorted idea. Both have been used to preach persistence, or perseverance, in prayer, but to draw that idea from these stories is to violate the text. The lessons intended by Jesus are to beget *boldness* and *assurance* when we pray—to ask freely and expect greatly.

In Luke 11:5-8, Jesus follows up His teaching on the Lord's Prayer by explaining the liberty one has in seeking help from a friend:

> Which of you shall have a friend, and go to him at midnight and say to him, "Friend, lend me three loaves; for a friend of mine has come to me on his journey, and I have nothing to set before him"; and he will answer from within and say, "Do not trouble me; the door is now shut, and my children are with me in bed; I cannot rise and give to you"? I say to you, though he will not rise and give to him because he is his friend, yet because of his persistence he will rise and give him as many as he needs.

Now, Jesus *didn't* intend what I'm about to describe, but I have heard this passage explained as though He meant to say, "Who of you is in bed at night, when a friend comes and beats on the door

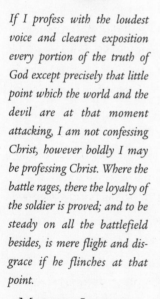

If I profess with the loudest voice and clearest exposition every portion of the truth of God except precisely that little point which the world and the devil are at that moment attacking, I am not confessing Christ, however boldly I may be professing Christ. Where the battle rages, there the loyalty of the soldier is proved; and to be steady on all the battlefield besides, is mere flight and disgrace if he flinches at that point.

MARTIN LUTHER
1483-1546

until broad daylight? Finally, you stumble out of bed, and say, 'Okay, if you are gonna beat on the door all night, then I'll get up and come down.' So beat on God's door until you get what you want!" The distortion suggests a picture of God as being bothered until He blesses.

But persistence as Jesus taught it doesn't have to do with an unrelenting beating on the door in prayer until God is awakened to your need.

Here's the picture He gives instead.

Jesus says, "Who of you has a friend, whose relatives unexpectedly arrive in the night? There is no food sufficient to feed them after their journey; and now they're at your door, knocking at a late hour and asking for your help. If this happened, would you say to your friend, 'Just keep beating on the door. . . . I'm really not interested in you, but I'll wait and see. If you keep pounding long enough, I might help'? Of course not!"

Jesus is teaching by contrast, showing what does *not* happen with us or with God. If a person knocks on your door at 3 A.M., you may not appreciate being awakened; but you're not going to get up and say, "Bug off! I don't need your wake-up call at this hour." Instead, as the Scripture says, you "will get up and give him as many as he needs."

Our Savior is saying something we all need to know about God and about how He feels when we ask Him for things we need: *He doesn't mind!* It's that simple. It's the lesson Jesus means for us to hear, so we'll persist in asking—continuously. Jesus presents this picture precisely to counter our human tendency toward hesitancy, to feel *My problems are too small to bother the Almighty*.

In the Greek language, "persistence" is *anaideia*. The prefix of the word, *an*, negates the related word *aidos*, which means "modesty, courtesy, reserve or propriety." In other words, the friend's persistence in waking somebody up in the middle of the night is a kind of *un*reserve, a challenging of social propriety. The asker didn't get his answer because he beat on the door until his fists were bloody but, rather, because he had the boldness to ask a friend—at night—and to directly relate a need. The nature of their relationship—friends—is what emboldened him to go and say, "Hey, I need help and I need it now!"

So Jesus is saying, "You have a Friend in heaven, and you don't need to be hesitant about asking." You don't need to be bashful about asking or worry about being appropriately reverent. Just ask. If there's a need, get at it! You don't need to be cautious in your approach to His almightiness!

Loved one, be done with the idea that God is nervous that you might ask something outside His will and with such energy that you will force Him into something He doesn't really want to do. He is saying, "Be bold. Don't be afraid to ask—anything!"

Jesus presents a parallel concept in Luke 18:1-5.

Then He spoke a parable to them, that men always ought to pray and not lose heart, saying: "There was in a certain city a judge who did not fear God nor regard man. Now there was a widow in that city; and she came to him, saying, 'Avenge me of my adversary.' And he would not for a while; but afterward he said within himself, 'Though I do not fear God nor regard man, yet because this widow troubles me I will avenge her, lest by her continual coming she weary me.'"

Before we read Jesus' conclusion, let's get a clear picture of the setting:

- This was a corrupt judge.
- He didn't care about God or man.
- He had no respect for either divine justice or earthly justice.
- But he still takes action in the interest of this widow because she keeps coming to him, asking that her case be handled.
- His motive is not justice for her.
- His motive (hardly noble) is that he is tired of being bothered by the woman.

Is Jesus making the judge a parallel to the Father? Obviously, no.

This is not a parable that teaches by *comparison* (as in the other story, which says, "Be bold like this"). Instead, this is a parable that teaches by *contrast*. Jesus is showing the opposite of the way things are with God.

Yet how many times I have heard otherwise? I've heard people interpret this story as though the Bride of Christ is like the widow, a woman with a tough case who can only get God (the judge) to act by persistent complaint. But Jesus means to show God's readiness, not His reluctance. Christ's prayer message in this passage is that we should expect God to take action—and quickly.

Here is Jesus' conclusion to the lesson:

> Then the Lord said, "Hear what the unjust judge said. And shall God not avenge His own elect who cry out day and night to Him, though He bears long with them? I tell you that He will avenge them speedily" (Luke 18:6-8).

Jesus points up the contrast between our Father in heaven—the just Judge—and a disgustingly inconsiderate, unjust human judge.

So where is the concept of persistence? Persistence according to Jesus is *not* the desperate extension of human energy, as though we're to labor long in an attempt to see heaven disposed in our interest. Nor does He show us a God "waiting in the wings" to see if we're really sincere; and after we have squeezed blood from the bedposts in frantic prayer, He will finally say, "Okay, now that you have proven yourself sincere, I'll do something."

That isn't God's way.

Instead, *the essence of persistence is recognizing that there is no situation to which you need surrender.* You can always ask your Friend in heaven. He will hear. You have a just Judge on your case. He'll act quickly.

Yet listen, dear friend. Sometimes the answers *do* seem long in coming. And when that happens, *know* that it does not reflect heaven's disinterest.

Sometimes a long labor—a period of travail—is required before we see the birth of what we have been anticipating. But be certain: The promise will be born. What may seem long on the earthly side of things is often but a moment in glory. So have patience.

Persistence is needed, but not as a humanly energized insistence that God see our sincerity or that we try and move God to action. He doesn't act on the basis of our zeal but, rather, on the basis of our simple faith and His changeless love.

God doesn't need to be moved to action. He's ready *now!* But to move mountains in this world often takes a season; so wait while heaven's bulldozers are at work, and find that the mountain *is* disappearing—a truckload at a time!

And as with the birthing process, so prayer's travail often involves a time of contractions. During that season, don't give up. Hold forth boldly and praisefully to see heaven break through with new life and victory in this world.

Even if time transpires, the mountain will move.

And even though hard labor may continue for a night—with tears—*joy* will come forth in the morning!

PRAYER THAT INTERVENES AND REVERSES

He is also able to save to the uttermost those who come to God through Him, since He ever lives to make intercession for them.

HEBREWS 7:25

The disciples' call to prayer is the call to a life of expanding dimensions—from worship to petition, from thanksgiving to warfare. As we've noted, Ephesians 6:18 points the way to:

- "praying always with all prayer" (that is, by every means of prayer)
- "and supplication" (literally, persevering for the promises, as contained in the text)
- "in the Spirit" (with supernatural assistance from Him).

Let me invite you—no, let me *urge* you—toward what's at hand. I want to discuss three grand words of prayer—"supplication," "intercession" and "thanksgiving." But I especially want us to see them in their relationship to that order of prayer I call *the prayer that intervenes and reverses.*

SUPPLICATION

In writing to the Philippians, the apostle Paul registered one of the broadest, most inclusive and most practical calls to prayer in the Bible:

> Be anxious for nothing, but in everything by prayer and supplication, with thanksgiving, let your requests be made known to God; and the peace of God, which surpasses all understanding, will guard your hearts and minds through Christ Jesus (Phil. 4:6,7).

Philippi was a Roman colony, an outpost of Rome's authority, and therefore secured with a special contingent of imperial troops. Paul's choice of terms, noting the *promise* of prayer, takes on special meaning in this light. He says, "The peace of God will guard your hearts and minds," the Greek word for "guard" describing the garrisoning of Roman troops to secure a colony. In other words, he was saying, "If you will take a specific stance in prayer, God will establish a stronghold in your mind, bracing you against the adversary so that you will never be cast into tumult or confusion, whatever your trial or need."

This text points the way for our entry into this place of secured confidence following prayer. But it involves more than simple petition—ordinary, give-us-this-day-our-daily-bread asking. Paul calls us to "supplication," an interesting word in the Greek language *(deomai)* that essentially has to do with "asking" but extends the idea further.

Strong's Concordance has linked in alphabetical sequence the words *deomai, deo* and *dei.* When I looked up the first, my discovery of these words in their natural *lexical* order helped me to see them in their *logical* order. First, their definitions:

- Deomai: "to supplicate or to make supplication; to beg; to pray earnestly"
- Deo: "to bind something up or to tie something up"
- Dei: a Greek particle, "ought"; used to express the moral imperative

The "moral imperative" refers to that which in the order of things "ought" to be. For example, if there's a need, we *ought* to help. If there's a fire, we *ought* to do something—help, warn someone, get water or even put it out. "Ought" means, in the order of things, "to do what's necessary and right."

Now, it was seemingly by accident that in discovering the linguistic relationship of these words, I was made to grasp the concept of supplication—that is, the pivotal difference between simply asking and supplicating.

To ask is to simply make our request known, and we've dealt with that already. But supplication answers to those times when a focused point of *passion* in prayer is needed. And when this need is joined to our recognition of the privileges we have been given in prayer, a distinct dimension of prayer is approached.

I had always been puzzled by "deomai" being translated "to beg" where prayer was involved, since Jesus does not *ever* teach prayer as begging. It doesn't reflect our relationship with God. But when we look at the cognate, "deo" ("to bind"), the dynamic between prayer and spiritual authority comes clearly into view. Consider Jesus' teaching regarding the authority His Church shall be given over the dark powers of hell:

> And I will give you the keys of the kingdom of heaven, and whatever you bind on earth will be bound in heaven, and whatever you loose on earth will be loosed in heaven (Matt. 16:19).

Therefore, it appears that "deomai" as a prayer exercise called supplication implies more than earnest begging. The evidence is that we are to see supplication as involving the Christ-authorized action of binding up certain things.

Understandably then, we ask, "What things do I have the *right* to bind up?" The answer, I believe, is in our seeing the cognate relationship of "dei" to "deomai." It would seem we are assigned to bind up things that are *not* what they ought to be and see them through in prayer until they *are* what they ought to be. Supplication, thus seen, is prayer that can return things to their intended order—to what is proper, or ought to be.

Look at our world, created under a divine order now long since violated. We understand that so much of our world is as it is, because the order God intended has fallen into confusion, chaos and disarray due to the fall of mankind, human sinning and satanic activity. Now, seeing things "out of order," God has ordained a "Mission: Possible" for we who have come under *His* order. We not only have the privilege of *fellowship* in prayer but also an invitation to *partnership* in prayer—to learn a dimension of binding by prayer unto the reconstitution of His original order and intent for peoples' lives and circumstances.

Supplication moves into the confusion of the fallen order of things (e.g., a broken heart, a broken home, someone's broken health) and begins through supplication to bind up broken things, drawing the strands of such binding back to what ought to be according to God's intent and God's will.

In short, the praying Church has been empowered by Christ's promise to pray in ways that stop what hell's councils are trying to advance.

This is what is meant by prayers that bind and loose. Binding is not limited to how we may conceive of something being tied up; it is also based on the concept of binding as it is used when a contract has been made. For example, when a property is being developed, an architect will regularly visit the site, meeting with the contractor to assure the details of the contract are fulfilled. Holding the contractor to the contract is legally possible because the terms of a contract are binding—but possible only as the architect or his representative insists on the "binding" clauses of the contract, ensuring that contested or neglected features of the project will be finished as they ought to be and as the owner wills.

The analogy is obvious. In this world, Satan is trying to construct things that are totally out of line from God's blueprint. You and I are on-site observers of what is taking place in human lives and earthly circumstances that we're made aware of. When what ought to be isn't, our role in supplication is to say:

> *Lord, what You contracted for at the Cross, for Your purpose*
> *and power to save [name] or deliver [name], isn't being*
> *done on Earth. Let Your ruling power, Your kingdom, come!*
> *Let Your will be done on Earth as it is in heaven. Lord, as*
> *Your agent assigned to this case in prayer, I say stop the*
> *adversary's advance. According to Calvary's terms, I "bind"*
> *the enemy from success. According to Your will through the*
> *power of Jesus' blood, I loose on Earth what You have*
> *already willed in heaven.*

Please notice that the grammar of the Greek phrase, translated in essence "whatever you bind will be bound, whatever you loose will be loosed," makes one thing clear that sometimes goes unnoted. It is important that we understand this fact: Our binding only accomplishes on Earth what has *already been* accomplished in heaven. In other words, we don't *make* things happen; prayer *releases* their happening. God has ordained the intended order so we are not creators of what occurs but rather *releasers* of what He has desired to be but which flesh or devil oppose. So when we bind or loose, remember, His is the power and the provision; ours is the privilege of participation.

Further, let us always be wise and praiseful, knowing the source of the power we exercise. Where does it flow from?

The Cross!

Never forget it, loved one. What Jesus did on the cross was once and forever to break the capacity of the adversary to sustain his rule over mankind. Apart from Calvary's power, we are no different. You and I have no defense in our own power. We're all helpless against Satan's strategies or contrivances, *except* that when we have the resources of Calvary, we not only have a sure defense for our own soul but also a point of appeal in calling for heaven's best in the face of hell's worst.

Because of Jesus' victory through the blood of His cross, prayers of supplication can bind—we can contract for heaven's ought-to-be deliverance and rejoice in seeing God's will done.

In this light then, it's not surprising that Paul said when we pray that way, the peace of God will guard our hearts. Prayer (asking) and supplication (binding and loosing) lay the groundwork for a deep peace to possess the soul if, as Philippians 4:6 says, praises of thanksgiving are offered with them. Faith brings peace, and anxiety will cease. Prayer has found a place of confidence by calling on heaven's resource and victory and by applying them in simple faith. Then with thanksgiving, we rest in praise as heaven's power moves to actuate the holy will and purpose of God's intended order on Earth as in heaven. The things we've addressed in prayer are set forward in Calvary's power of release, for God's glory and in Jesus' name. Amen.

INTERCESSION

Continuing with "all prayer" as our goal, let us look at the idea of intercession. Considering the apostle Paul's admonition in

1 Timothy 2:1-3, it's important and impressive to see the priority this order of prayer is given along with supplication:

> Therefore I exhort first of all that supplications, prayers, intercessions, and giving of thanks be made for all men, for kings and all who are in authority, that we may lead a quiet and peaceable life in all godliness and reverence. For this is good and acceptable in the sight of God our Savior.

Of particular significance is the *place* and the *scope* indicated—the priority ("first of all") and the aegis of influence ("for kings and all who are in authority"). In this foundational New Testament call to intercession, we have what I believe is the Bible's fundamental realm of assignment with regard to civic and political affairs. The directive is to pray for civic issues that are grander and broader than our own immediate points of personal concern or involvement. Obedience to this call will disallow any notion or practice of prayer as a preoccupying, self-centered concern. We are promised influence that can affect the climate of a culture ("that we may lead a quiet and peaceable life").

Understandably, it would be tempting to say, "Who am I to suppose that when I kneel, I can decide the moral, spiritual, political, military or economic circumstances in my country? In my world?" But the Word of God not only says intercession has that capacity, it specifically says intercession is one of our *first* assignments—a priority which, if observed, can reveal the living Church's real role in determining government. (While I believe a Christian in a free society should vote and be as politically active or involved as he or she feels called, the Bible says little about direct political control. Yet it has *much* to say about the intercessor's role in praying for governments.)

In James 5:16, the Bible notes, "The effective, fervent prayer of a righteous man avails much," and then provides an illustration of such prayer. The text, freely translated, reads, "The spiritually energized prayer of an impassioned person seeking God will count for more than he or she can imagine. Look how!" Then the case of Elijah is described:

> Elijah was a man with a nature like ours, and he prayed earnestly that it would not rain; and it did not rain on the land for three years and six months. And he prayed again, and the heaven gave rain, and the earth produced its fruit (Jas. 5:17,18).

A study of the Old Testament text being referenced here (1 Kings 17:1; 18:1-46) reveals a dramatic story of social, spiritual, economic and yes, meteorological impact through one man's intercession. The climate

But lo' the snare is broke, the captive's freed,
By faith on all the hostile powers we tread,
And crush through Jesus' strength the Serpent's head.
Jesus hath cast the cursed Accuser down,
Hath rooted up the tares by Satan sown:
All nature bows to His benign command,
And two are one in His almighty hand

CHARLES WESLEY
1707-1788

of the culture was *literally* changed, as drought conditions gave way to life-giving rain. The same passage shows Elijah's victory over the prophets of Baal—a spiritual triumph—and the breaking of a drought, which would have had obvious economic and social impact. God's judgment on the people was reversed, and this magnificent passage in James says that same potential is available today.

The broad, sweeping possibilities of intercession are unfolded in an examination of the Greek and Hebrew words used to indicate this type of prayer. *Entynchano* (Greek) and *paga* (Hebrew) have essentially the same meaning—a definition that seems peculiar to most when first heard. Both mean to "light upon," "come upon by accident" or "strike" (as lightning, unpredictably). Maybe you're like me, and your first exposure to those definitions evoked a bit of bewilderment. *Prayer by accident?* Let me give some examples of the use of paga in the Old Testament to demonstrate the awesome truth in this word.

In Genesis 28, Jacob is seen in flight, running from his brother, Esau. He comes to a place that will eventually be named Bethel. As he arrives there, he looks for a place to rest. During the night of sleep, he had the vision known as Jacob's ladder. When he awakened the next morning—after God met him in a dynamically powerful way, giving him a promise for his whole future—Jacob says, "Surely the LORD is in this place, and I did not know it" (Gen. 28:16). However, the day before, when he stopped at that site, the Scripture says, "He lighted upon a certain place" (v. 11, *KJV*). In other words, to Jacob's eye this was a random place of stopping; but in God's plan, it would become the milestone of his life.

Therein lies the idea of intercession. What seems random—catching us unexpectedly in time and circumstance and commanding our attention—is not accidental but *providential*.

Dear one, almost every day of our lives, you and I step into apparently random situations. If we perceive they are ordained of the Spirit, we will learn to respond to them, knowing God has brought us to them. There will be occasions when we will have a seemingly random thought, or a "signaling," which might seem accidental; but wisdom will teach us to seize these moments as intended by God to cause us to intercede for someone or some situation.

The issue of intercession does not have to do only with grand national and international issues, as we have already reflected upon, but also with anything that the Lord places before us as a point intersecting our daily lives. Perhaps you are driving along and see an accident in the roadway. Recognize that in God's providence, He has you present to intercede.

Please capture the divine significance of this for a moment. In many cases, you and I are the only people He has on the scene who have sufficient spiritual sensitivity to know that we can make a difference. The Lord wants to salt all of society with people who have this understanding—people who recognize that, as intercessors, they are present for the purpose of travailing in prayer for a world that otherwise would experience only the tragic consequences of life's problems, without the hope of divine entry to their circumstance through intercession.

Intercession occurs when people realize God has ordained boundaries of blessing for human experiences; and unless someone prays, Satan will try to violate the boundary line. He will try to make the experience less than it would have been in God's counsel and covenant. Intercession sees that God's purposes reach all the way unto what He wills. Unfortunately, there is a passivity that inhabits the mind-set of so many of God's people. It's kind of a spiritual sloth that causes us to think, *Well, God is all powerful. He can do whatever He wants and I'll sort of agree to it. Isn't that what "Thy kingdom come, Thy will be done" means?*

No, dear one.

Jesus taught us to pray "Thy kingdom come, Thy will be done" on this earthly side of things. Therefore we, the redeemed troops, are here to fight the good fight and to see heaven's covenant established and extended in the name of the King. We are not praying, *Oh, well, I guess "Thy kingdom come and Thy will be done."* Instead, we are praying, *I stand as heaven's ambassador on this planet. And I say, "God's kingdom come here, in this setting, and God's will be done."*

Intercession is insisting on the extension of heaven's covenanted boundaries, which hell will encroach upon and try to push back to less than what God has intended. We are the ones appointed to monitor the situation. In prayer we represent heaven's *purposes,* by heaven's *power,* speaking heaven's *covenant* into the situation; and we watch God actuate it according to our calling upon Him.

Paga occurs another place, in 1 Samuel 22. During the time of his backsliding as king of Israel, Saul was offended by some of the priests. He ordered his own troops to fall on them and kill them, but his troops respected God's priests too much to obey their own king. It was an embarrassment to him, so Saul turned to a pagan man, Doeg the Edomite, who had joined his entourage, and said, "Turn thou, and fall upon the priests" (1 Sam. 22:18, *KJV*). The hateful Edomite seized the moment, grabbed a sword and began to lop off the heads of God's priests. The Bible says that Doeg "fell upon [paga] the priests" (v. 18, *KJV*).

Now I admit that the scene is tragic—the slaying of God's priests. But the verb, objectively used in this setting, represents a person who goes on the attack, falling upon the perceived adversary of his king. It's a lesson in intercession, except in our case, our adversary is the devil, who "walks about like a roaring lion, seeking whom he may devour" (1 Pet. 5:8). In intercessory prayer, you and I are taking the sword of the Spirit and, at the direction of our King, falling upon the adversary, cutting off his efforts to attack and stopping his advance.

Intercession is such a dynamic form of prayer. It involves our ensuring on Earth the boundaries of God's heavenly purposes, defending against the enemy's encroachment, recognizing our privilege to take action at apparently random encounters and "controlling the climate" of societies and nations.

So how do we exercise the role of intercessor? In Romans 8:26,27, we read how the Holy Spirit is available to help us in this prayer dimension:

> Likewise the Spirit also helps in our weaknesses. For we do not know what we should pray for as we ought, but the Spirit Himself makes intercession for us with groanings which cannot be uttered. Now He who searches the hearts knows what the mind of the Spirit is, because He makes intercession for the saints according to the will of God.

Note the proximity of these two verses to the oft-quoted Romans 8:28: "And we know that all things work together for good to those who love God, to those who are the called according to His purpose." This much-loved verse must never be removed from its context!

Listen to me, dear one: All things *don't* work together for good in this world—not automatically! *Nothing* works together for good in this world on its own.

Romans 8:26-28 needs to be considered as a whole, for it shows how when intercessions energized by the Holy Spirit are brought to bear upon situations we don't understand, *then* there comes the entry of God's purpose—at which point "all things work together for good." But intercession is the pivot point determining *if* God's good will penetrate all things.

As that occurs, and we partner with Him in understanding and undertaking our prayer role, we allow the likeness of His Son to be developed in us.

Jesus' likeness is not only one of character; it is also one of spiritual authority. Jesus not only walked in purity of conduct, but He also walked about setting straight things that had been corrupted by the works of darkness. Remember Acts 10:38: "How God anointed Jesus of Nazareth . . . who went about doing good and healing all who were oppressed by the devil." Jesus was not just a good man. He was *God's* man. So as the Lord calls us to be conformed to the image of Christ (see Rom. 8:29), learning Holy Spirit-assisted intercession is a part of our character growth in Christ—a part of being conformed to His image as disciples.

THANKSGIVING

Finally, learn the power of thanksgiving!

> Rejoice always, pray without ceasing, in everything give thanks; for this is the will of God in Christ Jesus for you (1 Thess. 5:16-18).

The Bible doesn't say everything is a thank-worthy thing. It says, in everything you *see* be thankful. For example, if you saw the flames of a small brush fire threatening your home, you wouldn't stand there and say, "Thank God!" Instead, you would grab a rug to beat the fire out or spray water to drench it. But when hell's fire begins to draw near through tough or painful circumstance, the Bible says to use praise and thanksgiving—to God for His almightiness—to strike down the blaze.

We're not told *for* everything give thanks but rather *in* everything. That is, in the middle of everything, however desperate, *give thanks!*

How? Go out and begin slapping down hell's flames with praise to God. Shout to the high heavens that God is able to master this situation by His dominion, which you welcome with your worship. Say:

- I thank God this situation can't master us.
- I thank God He is bigger than what is happening right now.
- I thank God that though I had this accident, He is going to move into this scene and assist me.
- I thank God that though my sister has been diagnosed with cancer, we have a living Lord who is going to sustain us.
- I thank God that though I seem to be weak in my body today, He has promised me His strength and resources.

In everything, give thanks!

This is what Paul is saying when he writes, "For this is the will of God." Are cancer, difficulties and accidents the will of God? No. But the *spirit of thanksgiving* is the will of God concerning you.

As we look at worship, petition, supplication, intercession and thanksgiving, we are seeing some of the exceeding wonders of prayer for application in our personal lives, as we live in the power of the Spirit as growing disciples of Christ.

THE PRACTICE OF FASTING

As they ministered to the Lord and fasted, the Holy Spirit said,
"Now separate to Me Barnabas and Saul for the work to which I have
called them." Then, having fasted and prayed, and laid hands
on them, they sent them away.

ACTS 13:2,3

We shouldn't leave the subject of the exceeding wonders of prayer without dealing with the remarkable power of prayer joined to fasting. But when we deal with the subject of fasting, we not only encounter its unusual potential for spiritual dynamic, but also a couple of unusual problems.

First, believers can become confused regarding fasting, as though it were done to generate an energy born of our own exercise, as though fasting were a means of earning something from God. But the dedication and devotion involved in any exercise of prayer, including fasting, never has anything to do with our *getting* from God or "forcing" God into action. Rather, prayer and fasting are means of aligning ourselves with His possibilities of power through applying His principles of obedience in order to participate in His promises.

Second, the subject of fasting raises the problematic question for some people as to whether it is even relevant, necessary or important today. Some have suggested that it isn't, relegating fasting to the realm of the archaic, as though it is some medieval form of legalistic church tradition—people doing penance in an effort to purge themselves before God's eyes by punishing their bodies through fasting.

But notwithstanding these points of misunderstanding, the Bible speaks very clearly and pointedly about fasting being a part of a Christian disciple's practice. Hear it from Jesus' own lips:

> Then the disciples of John came to Him, saying, "Why do we and the Pharisees fast often, but Your disciples do not fast?"
>
> And Jesus said to them, "Can the friends of the bridegroom mourn as long as the bridegroom is with them? But the days will come when the bridegroom will be taken away from them, and then they will fast" (Matt. 9:14,15).

Jesus says, "As long as I'm here, this isn't the time for fasting, but when I am gone . . . yes." He's referring here to the season from His ascension until He returns again. Thus, in plain words, Jesus not only *allows*, but seems to *appoint* fasting as a Christian discipline.

Further, Paul enunciates fasting as a vital part of the life of a servant of Christ. In describing his own practices "in fastings often" (2 Cor. 11:27), he verifies two things: (1) He made frequent application of fasting, and (2) he didn't fast according to a calendar. He conveys the *rightness* of the discipline without a requirement of *ritual*. In short, the Holy Spirit can and will direct us to times of fasting.

There are seasons of fasting observed in some church traditions, and I certainly don't mean to devalue their observance or think them unwise. But I don't believe the individual is a failed Christian if he or she does not participate in these. Nevertheless, the discipline does beg the question: When might I fast?

In our congregation's life, many of us choose to fast for at least two meals every Wednesday. According to Wesleyan tradition, John Wesley and his followers fasted every Wednesday and Friday, from morning until afternoon tea at 4:00.

A BIBLICAL DISCIPLINE

Fasting as a discipline isn't meant to simply demand obedience of my body by submitting to this affliction of no food. Rather, it should be done as an active response to the revelation of the Scriptures on the subject.

The Bible shows fasting as having played a powerful role in some very dramatic and dynamic situations. The fact that many of these are Old Testament examples should not in any way discourage our taking them seriously for today:

> For whatever things were written before were written for
> our learning, that we through the patience and comfort
> of the Scriptures might have hope (Rom. 15:4).

Clearly, we're told in the New Testament that Old Testament principles are for our instruction, and we're wise to observe those that apply to our lives as Jesus' disciples. Let's look at four examples in the Old Testament in which the faithful fasted in situations similar to our circumstances today.

FOUR LESSONS TAUGHT FOR TODAY

And they mourned and wept and fasted until evening for Saul and for Jonathan his son, for the people of the

LORD and for the house of Israel, because they had fallen by the sword (2 Sam. 1:12).

Fasting at Transition

Saul and Jonathan had been slain. Because Israel had lost her leader and heir to the throne, David exercises a time of fasting and seeking the Lord. David eventually became ruler over all the tribes of Israel. The significance?

Consider the wisdom of people humbling themselves in the face of a successful attack by their adversary. Then consider the way you could apply a fast at a personal level or group dimension when destructive events assail your life. As you do, seek the Lord and expect the same result to be manifest—only now it will be the *Son of David* who will rise to rule over your circumstance.

Fasting for Survival

In Esther 4:16, the queen called her own people to fast. In essence, Esther tells Mordecai, "Go to the Jewish community and tell them to fast, and I'll go before the king and plead their case." The story is a crucial one in Jewish history. The life of the nation was on the line. As we study the flow of human history, we understand that such moments are more than merely political affairs; they are deadly, satanic attacks, as are any efforts to destroy an entire people!

Here Esther takes her place in fasting and her posture in intercession. As she goes before the king, behind her approach was a people who were fasting and seeking God. Similarly, there are times when we face situations where seemingly everything is at stake. But by seeking the Lord with fasting and intercessory supplication, we can discover His way to reverse the situation and see God's rule and grace enter in.

Fasting for the Future

Read Ezra 8:21-23 and see how great projects are best undertaken by the preparation of fasting and prayer.

The exiled Jews were preparing to return to Jerusalem with a large contingent of families and their valuables, including precious implements for reinstating worship in the Temple. Ezra, their leader, says, "I didn't have the nerve to go to the rulers who were releasing us and ask for soldiers to accompany and protect us on our journey." He knew the pagan onlookers were already marveling at how God was working on his people's behalf (see Ps. 126:1-3); to request human protection would seem to suggest that God couldn't do the job.

But Ezra does do something: He calls the people to fast, "that we might humble ourselves before our God, to seek from Him the right way for us and our little ones and all our possessions" (Ezra 8:21). Listen to it! There is something tender in these words, as a man describes a people seeking God's protection for, and guidance into, the future. They were fasting to make the transition to where God was taking them.

Sound familiar? Are you seeking a new time in your life? Are you looking for God's protection and leading as you navigate a present opportunity? Seek Him with fasting and prayer! And remember, Ezra focused not only on today's need but also on the way this action would serve future generations—our little ones.

Fasting and Spiritual Warfare

The Lord had revealed to Daniel great prophetic promises,

grand disclosures of His purposes. But the prophet says, "They were a long time in coming about" (see Daniel 10:1). (The message was true, but the appointed time was long.) The prophecy wasn't coming to full realization, and that's why Daniel begins to seek God with fasting and prayer.

Please notice that fasting is not something that is exercised apart from impassioned prayer. We've spoken about supplication, intercession, thanksgiving, petition and worship. You'll discover that most of these practices are evident in Daniel's prayer in 9:1-19. It's an extensive, intensive prayer—but notice also it's joined to a fast.

Fasting and prayer go together. Fasting without prayer is simply going without food. Is is not "foodlessness" but prayer—seeking God—that makes fasting powerful. We're not on a hunger strike, protesting God's inactivity. Dark spiritual powers are resisted and broken through fasting. As Daniel sought the Lord, God's purpose was released and a prophetic promise fulfilled—the prophetic promise of the termination of Israel's Babylonian exile!

Can you imagine how many situations today are awaiting someone who will recognize that God's time for deliverance has come? How many people "exiled from God's purpose" might be released as *we* fast and pray unto that objective?

NOTHING BUT PRAYER
AND FASTING

In Mark 9:29, Jesus is speaking to His disciples about a circumstance they had found themselves incapable of handling. When Jesus returned with Peter, James and John from the Mount of Transfiguration, He found the other disciples frustrated with their unsuccessful efforts to cast out a demon from a local boy. They asked, "Lord, why couldn't we do it?"

> So He said to them, "This kind can come out by nothing but prayer and fasting" (Mark 9:29).

Please note this text in your Bible, because I regret to tell you that some contemporary translations do not contain the whole verse. Some scholars have judged it to be insufficiently supported by manuscript evidence to retain it. However, the fact of the matter is there is virtually as much manuscript evidence to support the phrase "and fasting" as to omit it!

In *The Expositor's Greek Testament*, Dr. O. Morrison notes:

> The authorization for omitting "and fasting" with prayer because of its absence in some ancient manuscripts, really is not sufficient. But even if it were overwhelmingly so, fasting would in its essence be implied in this text.[1]

In other words, "and fasting" should not be omitted, but in any case fasting is at the very least implied. I press this point because I fear some may feel that its omission in some translations suggests fasting isn't important, even though Jesus said His disciples would exercise fasting as an abiding discipline until He comes again.

It is important that we recognize the power of fasting for breaking yokes of spiritual darkness. Remember, fasting is not about *earning* things from God but is for *learning* things from Him. And specifically, through fasting we can learn a realm of spiritual authority over the adversary which I don't think we will be able to explain until someday when we are on the heaven side of things. But Jesus does make it clear that fasting—with prayer—holds a dynamic that breaks evil power: "This kind only comes out this way!"

I don't know why, but somehow while I seek God, fasting drains hellish powers of their capacity to withstand the entry of God's kingdom. Jesus has said it, and that's enough to know. So let's learn from this event—and the other pivotal and practical illustrations the Scriptures give—of the power of fasting as a discipline.

PRACTICAL GUIDELINES

Now a few words of counsel on how to observe the fast. Simply stated, to begin it requires just plain good sense. And as I have already said, it involves frequent prayer. But people often ask other very practical questions—for example, "How long shall I fast?"

Only the Holy Spirit can direct you regarding the length of your fast, but practical considerations ought to be kept in view. Begin by asking the Lord to lead you as to how long your fast should continue. Some people's work requires such a heavy energy expenditure that it may not allow for a total fast. Remember, Jesus' 40-day fast wasn't carried on while He was keeping office hours or working at the plant every day. He went into the wilderness and was completely away from it all during that season of fasting. A day's fast as a regular discipline is the practice of many. Also, the three-day "believer's fast" has a long history in the Church.

When Daniel went on his 21-day fast, the Bible says he took "no pleasant food" (Dan. 10:3). The concept is that he didn't satisfy his appetite; he only ate enough to sustain himself. This was a voluntary reduction of intake, denying himself delicacies yet still answering the basic need for energy. This is an acceptable fast—observed with a perfect spirit.

Further, because we are not trying to convince God of our worthiness but rather are simply observing a biblically taught discipline, it is not unspiritual to recognize there will be functional and practical considerations at the physical level and they ought to be understood. Here are a few.

First, don't fast if there are medical or dietary reasons that prohibit it. One of my dearest mentors, a man now with the Lord, was a diabetic; yet Dr. Vincent Bird, my first bishop and lifelong friend, said to me a number of times, "When the congregation fasts, I've learned how to be in the *spirit* of a fast." By this he meant that he applied it with his heart, seeking God in a special way that only he could describe. By reason of his diabetes, he obviously needed to keep eating; but he

I was also led into a state of great dissatisfaction with my own want of stability in faith and love. . . . I often felt myself weak in the presence of temptation and needed frequently to hold days of fasting and prayer . . . that would enable me efficiently to labor.

CHARLES G.
FINNEY
1792-1875

still moved into the ministry of prayer with a special spirit—in power, but also in practical wisdom. Don't ever be so foolish as to violate medically directed dietary requirements and then claim that some spiritual pursuit brought you to such folly.

Second, understand that your body needs water. As a normal requirement, you should drink at least eight glasses of water daily—but especially when you are fasting. Water is not a violation of your fast. When Jesus fasted the 40 days, the Bible says that "in those days He ate nothing" (Luke 4:2). This specific mention indicates no abstinence from fluids. So, keep in mind, even our miracle-working Savior needed water. (Incidentally, some of the most spiritual people I have known have suggested to me that a squeeze of lemon in the water when fasting is helpful. It helps the body to cast off impurities during the fast, assisting the body's cleansing.)

Third, some individuals, whose regimen can't tolerate a complete fast, may find that drinking fruit juice will help them to remain in the spirit of the fast. I'm not suggesting this procedure as an escape if the Lord calls you to a more complete fast; but recognize this as one way to diminish your food intake during an appropriate pursuit of a fast. And in this vein, those who for some reason may be unable to participate at all, but whose partner is fasting, can still sustain a partnership in the fast by giving themselves to regular times of prayer beyond their usual pattern. No condemnation should be felt by one for not fasting along with one's spouse or prayer partner.

Fourth, fasting should be joined to special times of prayer, praise and intercession. For example, during a fasting time, why not set five-minute prayer breaks each hour or devote an entire lunchtime to prayer and praise. Seek out brothers and sisters in Christ who will feel a partnership with your seeking God in such a fashion, but only if they feel it's their desire and not the imposition of some religious pushiness on your part.

Finally, spend extra time in the Word of God when fasting. David said, "Your Word is sweeter than the honeycomb" (see Ps. 19:10). Jesus said the Word of God is nourishment to the soul (see Matt. 4:4). So feed on it.

And as you fast, be further nourished in knowing the pleasure of obedience to God as you fast: "My food is to do the will of Him who sent Me" (John 4:34). Those simple words spoken by Jesus express a concept of nourishment that we can partake of, especially in times of fasting, as we seek the release of the power that comes through this basic Christian discipline joined with prayer.

BEYOND DISCIPLINES

My brethren, count it all joy when you fall into various trials, knowing that the testing of your faith produces patience. But let patience have its perfect work, that you may be perfect and complete, lacking nothing.

JAMES 1:2-4

There is in these days a subtle presumption that tempts us all at times. We're especially vulnerable to its proposition since we are surrounded by technologically sophisticated systems and time-management models. The tendency is to suppose that if we cultivate sufficient "systems" of discipline, we can master Christian living.

Some of us turn to books with the latest "faith formulas" that promise to bring us answers on demand. Others exercise the sacraments mechanically, presuming they "work" without a warm, personal faith being joined to them. Any number of sure-fire systems have been proposed over the years, but the wise disciple won't be duped.

In the last analysis, our spiritual life is one of simple, moment-to-moment dependence upon Jesus. *Alone!* However beneficial acquired disciplines will become, settling and advancing your walk with Him, no method, system or discipline will ever substitute for our *just being His*.

Nothing brings this to the foreground more dramatically than life's tough or spiritually dry times. No degree of discipleship will remove you or me from the unexpected or the undesired encounter with trial, temptation, warfare or soul-weariness.

Beyond discipline, there needs to be a resignation of transcendent principles—stepping-stones for slippery times, a road map for those surprising turns that take you into a temporary desert.

Don't fear such prospects. They happen to us all. And even in the desert, God has promised the possibilities of His presence, and the promise includes a transforming of the desert into a beautiful experience:

> The wilderness and the wasteland shall be glad for them,
> and the desert shall rejoice and blossom as the rose (Isa. 35:1).

To capstone our look at healthy disciplines in the life of the disciple, let me share with you some final thoughts regarding seasons of difficulty and hardship.

SEASONS OF TRAVAIL

Nearly 500 pastors had gathered for a conference on the island of Mindanao, in the Philippines. My denomination had invited me to be the speaker, and as the first evening's service began, I was deeply moved by a prompting of the Holy Spirit. I knew I needed to share something with those dear men and women who so devotedly carried on the work of Christ. But I feared their misunderstanding— for the Lord had shown me their hearts were hardened.

This was not to say they were rebels or stiff-necked people, but instead, that their hearts were hardened by reason of the fires of circumstances. The juices of their souls were dried up and had become cracked as soil without moisture, dry as a riverbed where the sun has evaporated the water.

I saw these lovely people, who had labored faithfully in the heat of the day, showing the signs of dryness as a result of their service to Christ. They had faced the fires of hell in battle, and dryness in such circumstances can bring a hardness, or crustiness, to any of us. This doesn't necessarily mean a person has been neglectful of their commitment to Christ and His service.

Dryness is an occupational hazard of a disciple. David wrote, "As the deer pants for the water brooks, so pants my soul for You, O God" (Ps. 42:1). David was a man who understood the weariness of battle and of long labor without opportunity for refreshing. At such times we come to a desperate sense of our need of God.

Having been in public leadership for many years, I have ministered to thousands of believers who had become just as dry. It's easy to become perplexed, confused and disoriented—to feel that something is so wrong with you (or you wouldn't be this way) that you begin to despair. In this environment, we become vulnerable to self-condemnation, failure, bondage or affliction. In those dark nights of the soul, recognize what has happened to you.

O God, You are my God; early will I seek You; my soul thirsts for You; my flesh longs for You in a dry and thirsty land where there is no water. So I have looked for You in the sanctuary, to see Your power and Your glory (Ps. 63:1,2).

Hungry and thirsty, their soul fainted in them. Then they cried out to the LORD in their trouble, and He delivered them out of their distresses (Ps. 107:5,6).

For the enemy has persecuted my soul; he has crushed my life to the ground; he has made me dwell in darkness, like those who have long been dead. Therefore my spirit is overwhelmed within me; my heart within me is distressed. I remember the days of old; I meditate on all Your works; I muse on the work of Your hands. I spread out my hands to You; my soul longs for You like a thirsty land (Ps. 143:3-6).

In times like these, how can I find the fountain and be renewed in the blessing of the Lord? The answer is in Revelation 22:17, as the Scripture calls forth to us all:

And the Spirit and the bride say, "Come!" And let him who hears say, "Come!" And let him who thirsts come. And whoever desires, let him take the water of life freely.

Dear friend, we're being invited to drink by the One who Himself is the Fountain of Living Water—but who also, while on the cross, cried out, "I thirst!" (John 19:28).

Let that sink in. Jesus understands those times when in the midst of such thirstiness, you also cry out, "My God, why have You forsaken me?" Our Savior is very familiar with our times of travail, when in our aloneness and dryness we cry out to God for refreshing.

I want to close with these thoughts, because there is a mistaken notion in a few minds that to lead a disciplined life is to attain an exalted, almost euphoric, state of accomplished spirituality. The corollary to this supposition is that struggles, trials and dry seasons become things of the past. But this just isn't so.

Times of travail—those dry, in-between seasons of the soul—are certain to happen to even the most mature among us. Recognizing how they happen can help us deal with them when they come. So let me give you eight reasons why and how dryness of the soul occurs.

1. No Reprieve from Sustained Seasons of Demanding Duty
Some time ago I was speaking with a friend who had resigned

his pastorate. In the midst of very real demands of a building program, personal extenuating circumstances and a physical affliction, he recognized his burned-out condition and knew it would be best for all involved if he stepped down.

When there's been no reprieve from sustained seasons of demanding duty, anybody is likely to dry out. This is not only true of busy pastors. I've seen women so drained by pregnancy— followed by postpartum emotional swings and the demands of a new baby in the house—that their spiritual life absolutely goes to seed. Business people go through economic fires that sap life's juices. In such times, a certain cynicism may threaten to take over: *Does anybody know? Does God know or care about my situation?*

Read Genesis 21 sometime.

Hagar had been driven out by Sarah. She was lost in the desert with her baby, the reason for her being driven out. She's looking around, wondering if it's all over for her and the child. Then, the Bible says, "God opened her eyes, and she saw a well of water" (Gen. 21:19).

The Lord has the same hope awaiting you, too. Whether your labor is as a worker serving in the name of the Lord or your wearying labor was in having a baby, that dryness came from sustained, demanding duty. It doesn't mean you're unspiritual, but the dryness does need to be answered by God's opening your eyes.

2. Tireless Assault of Unrelenting Temptation

A second source of dryness is *prolonged* temptation. One of the most demanding times in my life was a season when the adversary bombarded my mind with an unceasing fear of failure. This lasted for a period of nearly four months. I didn't do (and hadn't done) anything wrong, such as yielding to any order of temptation. I was steadfastly faithful to the Lord all that time. But I kept fearing the relentless barrage coming on my mind was somehow eventually going to take over and dominate my life, as the vicious attack seemed never to go away.

But *then*—the day came when the enemy was defeated, as the Lord showed me these ferocious assaults were actually fashioning for me a great reward.

> Blessed is the man who endures temptation; for when he has been proved, he will receive the crown of life (Jas. 1:12).

I can hardly describe the joy I felt: *Praise God, this struggle isn't all for nothing. There's a crown of reward I'm about to receive!* That rich promise became so releasing to me! Let it be so to you, too, when your soul is drained by prolonged assault.

3. Bewilderment over Personal Tragedy or Reversal

Our minds ask questions when something upsetting, tragic or overwhelming has happened. Blessing seems absent due to such invasions into our lives and circumstances. At such times, it's easy to conclude that something bad happened because "there's something wrong between God and me."

Oh, how the adversary loves to steal from us and then to slap at us—to strike us in the face as though we were the ones guilty for creating the environment for his hateful invasion. The bewilderment that follows can dry us out. Learn to lay before the Lord any personal disappointment, any crushing sense of failure or anything which has caused you the dryness born of reversal and the condemning questions that so often ensue.

4. Attempting Too Long to Be Strong Without Partnership

There is a certain nobility in devotion when we seek to carry a load on our own. The Bible *does* say each of us shall bear his or her own burden (see 2 Chron. 6:29; Gal. 6:5). But it also says

"Bear one another's burdens, and so fulfill the law of Christ" (Gal. 6:2). This strikes at the heart of the way some sincere people try to live: "Oh, I don't want to bother anybody with my problems." They act as though there is a noble quality in their single-handed stalwartness, going it alone.

But not so, dear one. If we attempt too long to be strong without partnering with one another, we are not only violating Scripture—we're also destined for dryness. The words "each one shall bear his own load" (Gal. 6:5) refer to our personal responsibilities. But the word "burdens" in "bear one another's burdens" is the word for *overload*. Whenever you're on overload, *say so!* Don't wait until you're so mad that you scream it to somebody or until you're ready to break in some other way.

About a year ago I spoke with a small group of men with whom I meet regularly. I said to them, "Guys, I need to tell you— I'm just about numb. I've gone on overload." I had become nit-picking and irritable, and my wife pointed it out—nicely but accurately. I needed people to pray for me, to partner with me for a breakthrough. I wasn't just making an excuse ("You'll have to bear with me and understand, I'm so busy"). Excuses don't make it. Honestly saying "I need help" *does*.

Within days I experienced an amazing turnaround. The numbness and dryness—that I had accumulated through the raw demands of duty—were gone.

5. Attacks of Antagonism, Hostility and Criticism

There will always be people in the Church who are quick to pass judgment, criticize and complain. Their "ministry" can bake any soul dry!

Several years ago when God had broken forth with unique revival in the place I was serving, one of the most beloved teachers from my Bible college training days turned against me. Though not mentioning me by name, he publicly attacked certain things that were happening to me as the blessing of God swept through our church.

Bitterness began to enter my heart. The sense of love for a man I had always respected now was being betrayed; and instead of my being *watered* by that love, I found myself being *scorched* by criticism. I began to respond in dryness until I found another fountain of God's grace to compensate for what had been taken from me. Forgiveness followed, but I learned the danger of dryness when you are unjustly attacked.

6. Serving Ourselves at a Sensory Level
Rather Than the Spiritual Level

When you're weary, it's wise to learn that relaxation alone won't completely minister to your needs. Both the spiritual *and* physical dimensions need rest, and we can only find rest in God.

I had gone on vacation, and I needed it! I remember how delightful it was to get away to the beach for a week with Anna and the kids. They were great days. But about the fourth day, when I seemed to be so relaxed and freed from pressure, I found I was feeling *empty*. As I thought about my good external feelings, I wondered about the hollowness I felt inside.

Then it occurred to me.

I hadn't read a word of Scripture for four days. I hadn't prayed a prayer. I hadn't once sung a song of praise. I was just kind of "getting away from it all." Without planning or saying as much, it was as though we were usually so involved with church, the Bible and prayer, that we didn't want to do anything especially "godly" for a while.

Does that sound awful to you? Sure it does, but forgive me— it's the way I felt. And it wasn't because I didn't love the Lord. It's simply that I was exhausted beyond feeling.

But I was "called back" by the inner hollowness that I felt. And through that experience I learned the futility of trying to recover at the physical and emotional levels of my life if I neglect the spiritual dimension of my life.

If the lesson speaks to you, accept it. This is not a plea for religious action when vacationing but rather a remembrance of our need of God—of relationship with Him. He's the Fountain that answers to our dry times.

7. Experiencing Doubts Without Bringing Them to Jesus

Do you suffer sieges when prayers seem unanswered, problems seem unsolved or a prophecy seems unrealized? We begin to doubt if God is hearing our prayers, so we back away and discard the promises He's given to us.

Don't wallow in doubt. Renounce it by taking every question to the Lord. He isn't offended by our doubts. Say, "Jesus, I want to talk to You about this. I don't understand."

You might not find an instant answer, but I think you *will* find the refreshing of His presence. "In Your presence is fullness of joy; at Your right hand are pleasures forevermore" (Ps. 16:11). It is impossible to remain dry for long—however doubt-ridden— when we choose to abide in the presence of the One from whom the springs of living water flow.

8. Neglect of Basic Disciplines of Spiritual Sustenance or Known Disobedience to Understood Directives of the Holy Spirit

We'll go dry if we don't pray, if we don't drink the water of the Word, if we don't praise and if we fail to lift our voices in song. Dryness is generated if I consciously pursue a path of disobedience.

One day not long ago, I was walking through the living room at the house and looked over at the piano. I happened to be feel-

After a soul has been converted by God, that soul is nurtured and caressed by the Spirit. Like a loving mother, God cares for and comforts the infant soul by feeding it spiritual milk. Such souls will find great delight in this stage. They will begin praying with great urgency and perseverance; they will engage in all kinds of religious activities because of the joy they experience in them. But there will come a time when God will bid them to grow deeper. He will remove the previous consolation from the soul in order to teach it virtue and prevent it from developing vice.

ST. JOHN OF THE CROSS
1542-1591

ing kind of weary at the time. (As you may know, I play the piano and have written some songs of Christian worship.) As I glanced at the keyboard, the Holy Spirit whispered to me, *You haven't been there for several weeks, have you?*

I immediately realized He was addressing the reason for my dryness and weariness: I hadn't taken time as I usually did to come before the Lord in spirit-refreshing praise. I accepted the prompting and turned to a time of worship, and shortly I was renewed and refreshed.

The neglect of basic disciplines of spiritual sustenance—prayer, the Word, praise—has a way of drying out any of us. It may not be a very profound observation, but the answer to the very frequently asked question "What's happening to me?" is simply this: You can't neglect the basics.

Times of travail come to every believer. They weary the body, dry the soul, taunt the spirit, exhaust the emotions, beget doubts in the mind and breed despair in the heart. All those things seldom happen at once, but the variety of points at which we're vulnerable are enough to bring us all to times of questioning: "How did I get here? How can I get out? What's wrong, God? Why can't things be different?"

When dryness besieges the soul, it can touch areas of our life in such a way that it seems God's presence has evaporated. And when that happens, don't think you're strange and don't accept the Liar's accusations; but do turn to the Fountain of Living Water—Jesus—and remember that *seasons of travail mean something is about to be born!*

> Sing, O barren, you who have not borne! Break forth into singing, and cry aloud, you who have not travailed with child! For more are the children of the desolate than the children of the married woman. . . . Enlarge the place of your tent, and let them stretch out the curtains of your habitations; do not spare; lengthen your cords, and strengthen your stakes. For you shall expand to the right and to the left, and your descendants will inherit the nations, and make the desolate cities inhabited. Do not fear, for you will not be ashamed (Isa. 54:1-4).

And to that great promise of new life where there has been barrenness, add one more promise from Isaiah's prophetic message:

> Ho! Everyone who thirsts, come to the waters; and you who have no money, come, buy and eat. . . .
>
> For as the rain comes down, and the snow from heaven, and do not return there, but water the earth, and make it bring forth and bud, that it may give seed to the sower and bread to the eater, so shall My word be that

goes forth from My mouth; it shall not return to Me void, but it shall accomplish what I please, and it shall prosper in the thing for which I sent it.

For you shall go out with joy, and be led out with peace; the mountains and the hills shall break forth into singing before you, and all the trees of the field shall clap their hands (Isa. 55:1,10-12).

THE CHILD AND THE LAMB

I now want to bring a brief postscript to these many hours that we have spent together around the Word of God, studying about our life in Jesus Christ our Savior and opening our lives to the ministry of the Holy Spirit. I trust these printed words have inspired you to pursue the Spirit-formed life.

As we have focused on the keys to a growing, expanding walk with the Lord, we have explored the prospects of discipleship and the fundamental disciplines for servants of Jesus, as well as the exceeding wonders of prayer and the certainty of obstacles. We've hoped to secure the principles for living a growing life in God's power and purpose. But as we finish, one thought remains—which to my mind is as fundamental and essential as any I know.

You've doubtless heard the verse quoted many times, "'Not by might nor by power, but by My Spirit,' says the LORD of Hosts" (Zech. 4:6). It's usually quoted in some dramatic or sensational way.

Naturally, I joyously praise God for those dramatic or sensational ways in which His power sometimes works. But, dear friend, the very quotation of that verse, when accompanied by a thunderous demonstration of praise for God's visitation and might, somehow misses the essential setting and the point of that promise.

The man to whom the promise was given—at a time of real difficulty—was Zerubbabel. The building project that he was seeking to lead—the rebuilding of the Temple in Jerusalem—was not going well at all. That's when the prophet Zechariah came to him and said, "Zerubbabel, this is God's word to you: 'Not by might nor by power, but by My Spirit,' says the Lord of Hosts."

I frankly don't think the Lord was saying, "Watch Me whip this thing together in one glorious miracle moment." Rather, it appears that He was saying to Zerubbabel, "I have a way that transcends what you are able to do. Just call upon Me for My grace to bring it about" (see also v. 7).

God's *grace,* available *for all our needs* and *for all our lifetime,* is the grandest promise of all. And it's joined to, and it flows from, the moment of forgiveness of our sin and the beginning of eternal life. Just as grace is the means by which we receive salvation, grace is the means for letting God work in His might and power for our lifelong walk with Him. The heart that learns this will grow to learn the spirit of the love of God in Jesus Christ.

Do you remember when Jesus spoke to His disciples and said, "You do not know what manner of spirit you are of" (Luke 9:55)? They were looking for a visitation of God to do a powerful thing, but He wanted them to learn to have a tender heart.

That tender, teachable, touchable way is the path to true power—to lasting, miracle-expecting, Christ-exalting power and blessing. And with that understanding, I want to leave you with two words: *child* and *Lamb.*

The Child

Jesus said, "Unless you . . . become as little children, you will by no means enter the kingdom of heaven" (Matt. 18:3). He was not so much talking about receiving the new birth and going to heaven as much as He was telling us to learn a childlikeness of heart, so we may enter into the dimensions of God's rule—His kingdom power and blessing in our lives.

He was saying that childlikeness is the way to maturity.

Does that seem a paradox of terms, "childlikeness" and "maturity"? Let me tell you what I've come to believe very deeply about spiritual maturity.

There is no such thing as "adulthood" in spiritual life.

I've become convinced that we only learn how to be more like a child if we're *really growing*—more like a child in tenderness, responsiveness, teachability, malleability and openness to correction by the Father through His Spirit and His Word. And as we humble ourselves like children before the Ancient of Days, though we might attain 80, 90 or 100 years of life, our wisdom is scant at best and our maturity of years but a fleck of dust on the face of all eternity. We will all be *forever* children, however wise we may seem to have grown through life's lessons.

The Lamb

Finally, as we come before the Lord in childlikeness, let us learn to be like the Lamb. Jesus said, "Do not fear, little flock, for it is your Father's good pleasure to give you the kingdom" (Luke 12:32).

Hear Jesus say, "It's lambs who take the kingdom."

And He should know.

For it is in His dying as the Lamb of God that He ultimately gained possession of all authority over Earth and heaven, even over death and hell. He became a *child* in Bethlehem, knowing redemption would be revealed through a *lamb* on a cross. So we who follow in His pathways as disciples are wise to ever and always pursue these: childlikeness and lamblikeness.

And as we conclude in the intimacy of this insight, may our integrity with the Child who became the Lamb work these things in our lives. And may God always grant, until the day we see Him face-to-face, that we live as *His* sheep who will one day stand before Him with praise saying:

Worthy is the Lamb . . . to receive power and riches and wisdom, and strength and honor and glory and blessing. . . . forever and ever! (Rev. 5:12,13).

Amen!

HOW TO RECEIVE THE FULLNESS OF THE HOLY SPIRIT

Everyone who thirsts for Christ's deeper, fuller work in their lives asks how it can be done. My personal feeling is that to tell someone "exactly how" to be filled is to risk substituting a man-devised formula for what Jesus wants to do Himself. He is both ready and able to satisfy your quest without help from anyone else.

So in the light of all I've said, my simple encouragement to you now is to go directly to Him. Bow before Him. Open to Him. Trust Him. And ask Jesus to fill you with the Holy Spirit.

There are several thoughts—words I have often used to help those who feel hesitant, fearful or in need of further instruction. But before I share those, could I first just invite you to pray?

Your own words are sufficient. But if you believe the prayer I offer here will help you, then make it your own. No matter how you pray, the way to be filled now is to come, thirsty and believing—for the thirsty will be filled and the promise is yours (see Matt. 5:6; Acts 2:39).

Come to Jesus, for He's the Baptizer and He wants to fill you (see John 1:33).

Dear Lord Jesus,

I thank You and praise You for Your great love and faithfulness to me. My heart is filled with joy whenever I think of the great gift of salvation You have so freely given to me, and I humbly glorify you, Lord Jesus, for You have forgiven me all my sins and brought me to the Father.

Now I come in obedience to Your call. I want to receive the fullness of the Holy Spirit. I do not come because I am worthy myself, but because You have invited me to come.

Because You have washed me from my sins, I thank You that You have made the vessel of my life a worthy one to be filled with the Holy Spirit of God.

I want to overflow with Your life, Your love and Your power, Lord Jesus. I want to show forth Your grace, Your words, Your goodness and Your gifts to everyone I can.

And so with simple, childlike faith, I ask You, Lord: Fill me with the Holy Spirit. I open all of myself to You, to receive all of Yourself in me.

I love You, Lord, and I lift my voice in praise to You. I welcome Your might and Your miracles. May they be made manifest in me—for Your glory and for Your praise.

I don't tell people to say "Amen" at the end of this prayer, because after inviting Jesus to fill you, it is good to begin to praise Him in faith. Praise and worship Jesus and simply allow the Holy Spirit to help you do so. He will manifest Himself in a Christ-glorifying way, and you can ask Him to enrich this moment by causing you to know the presence and power of the Lord.

Expect the same blessings in your life as were received by people whose lives were recorded in Scripture. The spirit of praise is an appropriate way to express that expectation and to make Jesus your focus by worshiping as you praise. Glorify Him, and leave the rest to the Holy Spirit.

RESOURCES FOR FURTHER STUDY OF THE DISCIPLINES

The following are additional print, audio and video resources available from Jack Hayford. These titles have been selected to assist you in your further study of each of the 10 basic Christian disciplines covered in this book.

THE FIRST DISCIPLINE: COMMITTING TO HEAR GOD'S VOICE

Qualifying for Currency (Mark 4:21-25). An exposition of the passage from Mark, elaborating the author's encounter with God's Word as it is related briefly in this chapter. Tape #954.

Secrets I Have Learned in Opening God's Word (Ps. 25:12-14). An excursion through personal lessons and principles learned over a lifetime of hearing God, fearing Him and discovering His heart. Tape #4053.

How to Receive Prophesyings. This three-part study is directed toward applying wisdom and caution in taking practical steps as you receive "words" prompted by the Holy Spirit. Tapes #982, 985 and 989.

THE SECOND DISCIPLINE: LIVING IN THE POWER OF BAPTISM

Newborn: Beginning Your New Life in Christ. This booklet contains practical guidance and counsel for the new Christian, including a section that answers questions regarding water baptism.

Believe and Be Baptized (Mark 16:16). A clear, pointed summons to obedience in water baptism, brought with a prophetic passion that calls those who have received Christ but have not yet been baptized to do so. Tape #2086.

Defining "All Righteousness" (Matt. 3:11-15). An insightful, expositional development of the three key points of release related to water baptism, as revealed in Jesus Himself. He who seemed not to need baptism did so for dynamic reasons that apply to us today. Tape #3505.

THE THIRD DISCIPLINE: CELEBRATING THE LORD'S TABLE

The Lord's Table in Your House. Biblical instruction on the place and power of partaking of the Lord's Table in the private setting and circumstance of one's own home. Tape #1415.

The Full Scope of Communion (Rev. 12:10,11). A look into God's provisions for spiritual deliverance, victory and triumph over the enemy, as the resources of the Lord's Table are understood and applied. Tape #1350.

Thanksgiving Table Manners (1 Cor. 11:17-34). A review of the apostolic intention in the urgings and warnings given concerning the Lord's Table shows how to untangle confusion, remove condemnation and release joy. Tape #4631.

THE FOURTH DISCIPLINE: WALKING IN THE SPIRIT OF FORGIVENESS

The Key to Everything. This full-length book from Creation House develops the principles of life stewardship being fully freed to develop in a disciple—in proportion to the disciple's learning and living in forgiveness.

The Spirit of Release (Matt. 18:21-35). An exposition and elaboration of the biblical text discussed in this chapter. Tape #2586.

The Fullness of Forgiveness (Luke 15). The glory of God's grace and the full dimension of our forgiveness in Christ are expounded from the biblical text relating the forgiveness and restoration of the prodigal son. Eight-tape album #SC 021.

The Device of Unforgiveness. This three-part series is a practical case study of the challenge faced in the Corinthian congregation. Learn to deal with the principle of self-administrated, interpersonal bondage that can result when the satanic ploy of legal enforcement blinds our hearts. Includes:

- Part I—2 Cor. 2:9-11 and 1 Cor. 5:1-8. Tape #1507.
- Part II—1 Cor 5:9-13 and 2 Cor. 2:10,11. Tape #1510.
- Part III—2 Cor. 2:1-11 and 1 Cor. 5. Tape #1523.

THE FIFTH DISCIPLINE: FEEDING ON THE WORD OF GOD

The New Testament (NKJV). Read by Pastor Jack Hayford, here is the complete text of the New Testament for listening as you work, drive, travel or meditate alone.

Breadbreaking. This audio study series presents practical steps for developing solid, sensible habits in reading and feeding on the Word of God. Includes:

- Bridging Pitfalls to Reading (Ps. 19:7-10). Tape #2679.
- Engraving the Word in Your Heart (Matt. 4:1-11). Tape #2684.
- Verifying Your Character Through Bible Study (2 Tim. 2). Tape #2687.

Believing in the Bible. This is a four-tape study dealing with the questions surrounding where we got our Bible and the intellectually satisfying and spiritually dynamic reality behind the trustworthiness and credibility of God's

Word as we have it in the Scriptures. Tapes #1855x, 1860 and 1905.

Which Translation Is Right? (Heb. 4:12). This presentation deals with the often-asked question "What translation should I use?" Here's a guide to the value of the different contemporary Bible translations. Tape #1900.

THE SIXTH DISCIPLINE: MAINTAINING INTEGRITY OF HEART

Honest to God. Penetrating insight that searches our hearts while lifting us to expect to "see" God's ways and works fulfilled in our lives. Part 1, "Integrity of Heart," is a study of Genesis 20:1-6. Part II, "Singleness of Eye,"covers Luke 11:33-36. Two-tape album #SC 122.

Repentance and the Kingdom. A six-tape study showing the power principle of repentance in its lifelong dynamic when applied with understanding, without condemnation and with consistency to the principles Jesus reveals in the Word. Includes:

- The Essence of Repentance (Luke 3:1-14). Tape #1621.
- The Edge of Repentance (Luke 3:9). Tape #1624.
- The Evidence of Repentance (Matt. 3:7-9). Tape #1627.
- The Elements of Repentance, Pt. 1 (Matt. 3:1-6). Tape #1635.
- The Elements of Repentance, Pt. 2 (Luke 3:3-6). Tape #1638.

• The Entrance of Repentance (Matt. 3:1,6; Luke 3:3). Tape #1643.

The Seventh Discipline: Abiding in the Fullness of the Spirit

The Spirit and the Glory. An 80-minute, five-segment video designed to be a teaching and ministry resource for personal or group use. Includes sensible, scriptural answers to common questions about baptism in the Spirit.

Spirit-Filled. This 90-page booklet published by Tyndale House defines the meaning of being "filled with the Holy Spirit."

How to Receive the Baptism of the Holy Spirit. This study of Matthew 14:22-33 shows the beautiful parallels between Jesus' invitation to Peter to "step into a miracle" (walk on the water) and the Savior's call to every believer to come to Him and receive the power that will enable us to live and serve Him in a supernaturally empowered dimension. Tape #0267.

The Beauty of Spiritual Language. This book published by Thomas Nelson deals with the God-intended, practical resources and the blessing inherent in the Holy Spirit's gift of "speaking with tongues." Written to respond to the many related questions and dealing with the *abuses* as well as the *uses* of a prayer language, answers are given, biblical guidance provided and spiritual hunger awakened to abide in Christ with comfort and confidence in the validity and functionality of this prayer, praise and intercessory help the Holy Spirit offers to us all.

The Problems and the Benefits of Spiritual Language. Here are four teachings spanning the multiple questions, confusing error, ugly violations and beautiful possibilities surrounding the subject of the valid, biblical practice of "speaking with tongues":

• The Problems (1 Cor. 14:30-38). Tapes #280, 286.
• The Benefits (1 Cor. 14:1-29). Tapes #287, 291.

THE EIGHTH DISCIPLINE: LIVING A LIFE OF SUBMISSION

Submission: The Key to Freedom (John 13:14-17; Heb. 2:1-12). This important two-part tape series presents sound-minded, Bible-based principles of submission. Tapes #0011, 0017.

Submission to the Body (Eph 1:15-23; 5:15-21). Tape #0014.

Submission in the Family (Eph. 5:22—6:4; 1 Cor. 11). Tapes #0018, 0019 and 0020.

Right Relationships and Dynamic Deliverers (Exod. 4:18-31). This five-part audio series provides insight into how submission, wisely understood, produces people who (like Moses) assist others toward true spiritual freedom. Tapes #701, 707, 711, 720, 753 and 760.

THE NINTH DISCIPLINE: PRACTICING SOLITUDE

Our Daily Walk. This 92-page booklet (formerly titled *Daybreak*) sets forth in written form the material covered in the following tape series. Published by Renew Books/Sovereign World.

The Renewal of Devotional Habit. This profoundly practical study series transformed a congregation, as three consecutive Sundays became a real-life encounter with the principles of establishing a pattern of daily personal devotion. You will find herein far more that what you "ought to do." Here's *how* to do it. Tapes #2178, 2180 and 2183.

THE TENTH DISCIPLINE: LIVING AS A WORSHIPER

Worship His Majesty. This classic 272-page book from Regal Books develops a study of worship as "the second Reformation," examining the principles of worship as they unfold through the experiences of personalities in the Scriptures.

The Heart of Praise. This 255-page devotional published by Regal Books is filled with key concepts undergirding life and congregational transformation through the application of central themes found in the book of Psalms.

The Uniqueness of Christ. This video message comes with a 40-page booklet and introduces us to the beauties of Christ. This study focuses on Jesus as the world's only Savior and Deliverer and deals with issues of Christ-centered evangelism. Video #UOC-V.

So Great Salvation. This five-part audio series is a sensitive, heart-moving inquiry into the wonders of God's gift of His Son to us. Pastor Hayford unfolds the love of God in Jesus, who came to meet us in our need. Audio album #SC 161.

You may order materials by title or catalog number through Living Way Ministries. For more information about these and other resources by Jack Hayford, contact:

Living Way Ministries
14800 Sherman Way
Van Nuys, CA 91405-2233
Phone: (800) 776-8180
Fax: (818) 779-8411
http://www.livingway.org

ENDNOTES

Fundamentals of the Spirit-Formed Life
1. "As Time Goes By," lyrics by Herman Hupfeld, 1931. The song endures largely due to the prominent role it plays in the 1942 wartime drama *Casablanca*, starring Humphrey Bogart and Ingrid Bergman.

The First Discipline: Committing to Hear God's Voice
1. "In the Garden," lyrics by Charles Austin Miles, 1913.
2. "He Lives," lyrics by Alfred H. Ackley, 1933.
3. Jack W. Hayford, *Moments with Majesty* (Sisters, OR: Multnomah, 1990), pp. 220, 221.

The Sixth Discipline: Maintaining Integrity of Heart
1. Carl Friedrich Keil and Franz Delitzsch, *Commentary on the Old Testament: Pentateuch*, vol. 1 (Grand Rapids, MI: William B. Eerdmans, 1971), pp. 198, 199.
2. Hayford, *Moments with Majesty*, pp. 221, 222.

The Seventh Discipline: Abiding in the Fullness of the Spirit
1. Let no one misunderstand me. I'm not recommending rebaptism as a "rite" but, instead, as an internal, open-hearted renewal in the reality and glory of the power God's Spirit brings to these experiences.

The Eighth Discipline: Living a Life of Submission
1. "Trust and Obey," lyrics by John H. Sammis, 1915.

The Ninth Discipline: Practicing Solitude
1. "As the Deer," lyrics by Martin Nystrom, 1984.
2. "In the Garden," lyrics by C. Austin Miles, 1912.
3. Hayford, *Moments with Majesty*, pp. 41-43.
4. Ibid., pp. 34, 35.

The Tenth Discipline: Living as a Worshiper

1. Hayford, *Moments with Majesty*, pp. 170, 171.
2. "Is Your All on the Altar?" lyrics by Elisha A. Hoffman, 1905.

Prayer Path, Step 10: The Practice of Fasting

1. *The Expositor's Greek Testament*, ed. W.R. Nicoll (New York: 1897).

REGAL BOOKS BY JACK HAYFORD

Built by the Spirit

The Christmas Miracle

The Heart of Praise

I'll Hold You in Heaven

Loving Your City into the Kingdom
(with Ted Haggard)

Pastors of Promise

Worship His Majesty

More Ways to Draw Closer to the Father

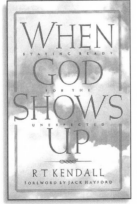

More From
Jack Hayford

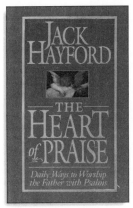

The Heart Of Praise
Jack Hayford
Daily Ways to Worship the
Father with Psalms

Hardcover
ISBN 08307.16092

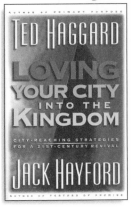

**Loving Your City Into
the Kingdom**
Jack Hayford and Ted Haggard
City-Reaching Strategies for a
21st Century Revival

Paperback
ISBN 08307.18958
Video
UPC 607135.001119

**The Basics of Deliverance
Volume 1**
Jack Hayford & Chris Hayward
The Multiple Means of
Deliverance & Preparing
the Masses for Deliverance

Video
UPC 607135.004660

I'll Hold You in Heaven
Jack Hayford
Healing and Hope for the
Parent Who Has Lost a
Child Through Miscarriage,
Stillbirth, Abortion or
Early Infant Death

Mass
ISBN 08307.14596

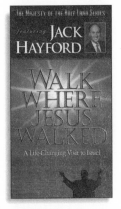

**Walk Where
Jesus Walked**
Jack Hayford
A Life-Changing Visit
to Israel

Video
UPC 607135.000785

The Christmas Miracle
Jack Hayford
Experience the Blessing

Hard Cover-Gift Edition
ISBN 08307.25180